Marketing Parks
and Recreation

National Park Service
Park and Recreation Technical
Service Division
Western Regional Office

Venture Publishing, Inc.

This publication was prepared by the
Park and Recreation Technical Services Division,
Western Regional Office of the National Park Service.
The client-oriented marketing content was authored by Howard Levitt;
the needs assessment content was authored by Dr. John L. Crompton,
Department of Parks and Recreation, Texas A & M University and
edited by Harry Williamson; and the power of promotion content
was written by John B. Goldsmith with Norman McKinnon as a contributor.

GV
181.43
.M37x

Library of Congress Card Number: 83-50125

ISBN 0-910251-07-X

Cover Design: Marilyn Shobaken

Illustration by ExecuTech, Hayward, CA

Foreword

Recreation providers, public and non-profit, are facing more difficult challenges than ever before. Most successful agencies and organizations are aggressively searching for new ways to confront problems. How an agency markets its programs or services has become critical to the management function. This book takes a new look at marketing - an orientation on which the survival of the agency or organization may depend.

Marketing is an often misunderstood concept. Many people assume that marketing is concerned solely with the promotion of programs or services. However, management experts from the public and private sector alike consider client-oriented marketing to be the key to successful and relevant programming, as well as to cost-effective operations.

All organizations market with varying degrees of sophistication and coordination. This book is dedicated to a marketing approach that is based on four discrete steps: analysis, strategy development, implementation and evaluation. Central to this whole approach is the assessment of need and a well-designed program of promotion.

Meeting the challenge of today's leisure service market has prompted many park and recreation agencies to adopt private sector practices. Increasingly, successful managers are turning to marketing as a means of providing their clientele (the public) with more relevant services at fairer prices, more efficient delivery of these services and enhanced program awareness.

Needs assessment tells the agency what the citizens see as the agency's mission and what they would like to see the agency do now and in the future. A discussion of ways to conduct needs assessments is presented, with special attention to the survey method.

Park and recreation agencies all over the country have conducted needs assessments of varying degrees of sophistication and with varying degrees of success. Examples of some of these are provided which are considered to be contemporary and exemplary in terms of their design, methodology and successful results.

In the promotional arena, attention is given to the design of a comprehensive promotion program for a park and recreation agency. And finally, no promotion book would be complete without tips on the four major promotion technique categories of publicity, advertising, personal contact and special promotions.

Therefore, this book is written for public and non-profit recreation and park agency managers who are interested in increasing user satisfaction, expanding clientele, increasing revenues, saving money and building a constituency.

Contents

Foreword iii

I   CLIENT-ORIENTED MARKETING
        An Orchestrated Approach to Meeting Your
             Clients' Needs 1

        Marketing--An Introduction. 3
           Marketing--What Is It?. 3
           Benefits of Marketing 3
           Dispelling Marketing Myths. 5
           Orchestrated Marketing. 6
           Section Profile 7

        Analysis. 8
           Section Profile 8
           Analysis. 10
           Data Collection 10
           Interpretation. 16
           Strengths, Weaknesses, and Opportunities. . 19
           Post-Audit/Analysis Tasks 19

        Strategy Development. 21
           Section Profile 21
           Strategy Development. 22
           Goal Setting. 22
           Targeting 23
           Designing a Strategy Mix. 24
           Product 24
           Price 25
           Promotion 30
           Distribution. 38

        Implementation. 41
           Section Profile 41
           Implementation. 41
           Gaining Consensus 42
           Responsibilities. 42
           Leadership. 43

        Evaluation. 46
           Section Profile 46
           Evaluation. 47
           Coda. 48

Appendices. 49
   Appendix 1--A Marketing Audit Outline . . . 49
   Appendix 2--Market Segmentation 54

Selected Bibliography 57

II   NEEDS ASSESSMENT
Taking the Pulse of the Public Recreation
       Client 61

Introduction. 63
   Why Do a Needs Assessment?. 63
   General Approaches to Needs Assessment. . . 64

Preparing to Do a Needs Assessment Survey . . 70
   Why Don't Agencies Make More Use of Needs
      Assessment Surveys?. 70
   What Do You Want to Learn from the Needs
      Assessment Survey? 72
   Which Survey Method Should Be Used to
      Collect the Information? 74
   How Much Will It Cost?. 78
   How Long Will the Survey Take?. 81
   Management of Interviewers. 81
   So Which Survey Method Should I Use?. . . . 82

Designing the Questionnaire 83
   Introductory Comments and the Cover Letter. 83
   In What Order Should the Questions Be
      Asked? 84
   Question Content. 86
   Question Phrasing 86
   What Type of Questions Can Be Used? 86
   What Does the Questionnaire Look Like?. . . 87
   Beware of "Motherhood" Questions. 88
   Pre-Test and Revision of the Questionnaire. 89
   Validity and Reliability. 90

Selecting the Sample. 92
   How Many People Should Be Selected for the
      Survey?. 92
   Sampling Methods. 93
   What Method Should Be Used to Select
      Respondents? 96

Completing and Evaluating the Survey..... 97
    Completing the Survey........... 97
    Evaluating Needs Assessment Studies.... 100
    Epilogue................. 101

Appendices.................. 102
    Appendix 1--A Checklist for Evaluating
        Needs Assessment Surveys....... 102
    Appendix 2--Sample Questionnaires..... 106
    Appendix 3--Samples of Cover and Follow-Up
        Letters............... 107

Selected Bibliography............ 110

III   THE POWER OF PROMOTION
    Techniques of Publicity, Advertising,
        Personal Contact, and Special
        Populations.............. 113

Designing a Comprehensive Promotion Program. 115
    Marketing Analysis and Strategy Development 116
    Identification of Promotion Goals and
        Objectives.............. 117
    Development of a Promotion Strategy.... 119
    Budgeting................. 120
    Implementation of Your Promotion Program.. 122
    Evaluation................ 123

An In-Depth Look at Key Promotion Techniques. 126
    Publicity................ 126
    Advertising............... 134
    Personal Contact............. 156
    Special Promotions............ 161

Selected Bibliography............ 169

I. Client-Oriented Marketing
An Orchestrated Approach to Meeting Your Clients' Needs

Marketing — An Introduction

MARKETING--WHAT IS IT?

Public sector marketing may be described as a set of activities which are aimed at effecting an exchange with clients. In a more basic form, marketing involves the development of services which are consistent with client needs, then pricing, promoting, and distributing those services effectively.

Marketing is performed in a variety of ways, including conducting user surveys; preparing descriptive program brochures; cordial reception and hospitality; responding positively and quickly to complaints; setting appropriate, equitable prices for services; maintaining facilities in good condition; and projecting a good image. Marketing reflects how an organization interacts with its clients and customers. An organization with an effective marketing program has as its primary goal the ability to meet the needs of its clientele. From this basic goal flow a number of benefits that strengthen and sustain the organization itself. Thus, both the client and the agency benefit.

BENEFITS OF MARKETING

Marketing begins and ends with the needs of the client. There are four ways that marketing enables you to serve your clients better:

    Relevant services

    Efficient service delivery

    Enhanced program awareness/better communication

    Fairer pricing

<u>Relevant services</u>. There is little room for irrelevance in service delivery. By providing relevant services, an organization strengthens its stature vis-à-vis other organizations competing for limited funding in the public sector, as well as in the nonprofit and private sectors.

In focusing all efforts on satisfying client needs, only those programs and services which most effectively accomplish that goal will be sustained. An effective organization will constantly strive to provide services which satisfy. New programs will be constantly evolving in response to new needs. Trends will be monitored and programs designed to catch the rising wave of popularity and not merely ride the foam after the wave has crested. This focus on needs satisfaction directly benefits your clients. Relevance in services is a tricky business. The landscape is strewn with poorly attended program casualties such as disco dance classes started too late or skateboard parks built after the trend had peaked.

<u>Efficient service delivery</u>. In creation, as in other aspects of life, it's better to accomplish fewer tasks well than many tasks poorly. As a part of marketing, an organization will assess its ability to provide a service efficiently. Effective marketing enables an organization to allocate finite resources for those activities that deliver in terms of the ultimate judge--the client. Through marketing, decisions of what to undertake and what to discontinue are made on a rational basis.

In some cases, efficiency may be best served by not offering a service. After reviewing its capability to provide recreation swim programs, the Community Services Department in Campbell, California, discontinued its swim classes. The department had determined that the YMCA could better provide swim classes. By dropping their swim classes, the Community Services Department freed resources for programs it could provide more efficiently. Clients wanting swim instruction gained, and the Community Services Department avoided the negative impressions that inefficient classes might have created.

Without the information gained through a market analysis, services may only partially satisfy a broad clientele. Marketing permits an agency to more precisely target programs for specific client groups, with a much greater likelihood of client satisfaction. This is another facet of marketing as a tool to enhance service efficiency.

<u>Enhanced program awareness/better communication</u>. Disappointing participation rates are often the result of a lack of awareness. In an effective marketing program, promotional efforts, like the services themselves, are targeted to the clients for whom the services have been designed, thereby increasing awareness and participation.

Services are advertised and publicized in a place and fashion that will reach the intended client groups. Lack of service awareness is a serious problem for many recreation organizations. Marketing principles can help combat the problem.

Fairer pricing. Pricing is an important aspect of marketing. It permits an agency to determine public support for a service and therefore helps the agency to determine the amount of subsidy a particular service should receive. This leads to a price that is fairer for service users.

Each of the client benefits described above translates into an agency benefit. Relevant, efficient, and well-promoted services result in greater user satisfaction, higher participation rates, increased revenues, improved staff morale, and greater support by decisionmakers.

A marketing philosophy . . .

1. Assures a focus on actual public needs and reduces the preoccupation with continuing traditional agency programs and services

2. Typically leads to a more appropriate and realistic definition of agency role and responsibilities

3. Encourages innovation, experimentation, and creativity in programs and services by suggesting there are a variety of ways to satisfy public wants

4. Is useful in promoting and justifying policies and programs to boards and elected officials

DISPELLING MARKETING MYTHS

For many public and nonprofit recreation practitioners, marketing remains a misunderstood concept. For some, the very word "marketing" evokes unsavory images. Marketing is not a negative concept. It is a client service orientation which is commanding new interest in the public sector. Several common marketing myths are examined briefly below.

MYTH: Marketing and selling are the same thing. Marketing is a broad concept, encompassing a large number of activities. Among those activities are promotion and personal selling. Selling is related to marketing in much the same way that the voice relates to communication. Before words are spoken, the mind has already assessed the need for communication, has conceived an appropriate message, and has determined that the voice is the most effective way to communicate the message. Finally, the mind activates the vocal chords to produce a sound. Selling is one of the voices of marketing, activated only after a series of research and planning phases of the marketing process has already occurred.

MYTH: Marketing is an expensive luxury. The annual marketing budgets of major corporations run into the millions of dollars because corporate decisionmakers consider marketing a necessary investment. For public agencies and nonprofit organizations, marketing is no more of a luxury than it is for a Fortune 500 corporation. Marketing brings together activities that all organizations undertake, with the goal of effective client service.

Decisions based on sound marketing principles can often save an organization money since decisions are made with a knowledge of what will and will not contribute to service effectiveness. Wheel spinning and ineffective, marginal-return approaches can be minimized. In addition to the savings attainable through more efficient delivery, an organization can realize a higher return on revenue-generating activities and facilities through the use of proven marketing techniques.

Many marketing activities cost little or nothing. A positive image, reinforced by a courteous, well-informed staff, can be developed at a very low cost. A smile, a pleasant telephone manner, a prompt response to inquiries--these are some of the cost-free essentials of a good marketing program.

MYTH: Marketing is manipulative and self-serving. Some people conjure up visions of clever but unscrupulous program designers playing on the sympathies and emotions of the unsuspecting public to get them to buy services they really aren't interested in. In the public and nonprofit sectors especially, marketing is exactly the opposite of manipulation. In a marketing approach, the main concern is understanding the desires of the clients and serving these desires with relevant, cost-effective services. The client is the boss and the client directs the organization, not the other way around.

ORCHESTRATED MARKETING

For marketing to be most effective, it's important that it be integrated into every facet of your organization's operations and orchestrated properly. For this reason, the components of a marketing process can be likened to a symphony orchestra. Just as symphony orchestras are arranged in sections, there are four distinct sections of an orchestrated marketing program:

   Analysis

   Strategy development

   Implementation

   Evaluation

Each section of a symphony orchestra contributes in its own way to producing a harmonious rendering of the musical program. So do the sections of a marketing program blend and interact to produce products and services that please the intended audience.

The marketing process described in this handbook is a synthesis of a number of processes at work in the public, nonprofit, and private sectors. Our goal is to simplify marketing into a four-phase process that is applicable to specific programs and services, as well as to an organization's overall operations. Those managers whose organizations already employ a coordinated marketing process should readily recognize their approach within the processes described in this handbook.

SECTION PROFILE

Each of the next four chapters begins with a SECTION PROFILE. The Section Profile services as an outline for the discussion which follows in the chapter. The profile highlights:

Marketing Role: What function does this aspect of marketing serve in helping the organization better serve client needs?

Instruments: What are the specific components of the section?

Techniques: How or through what means is this phase of the marketing process accomplished?

Conductor's Concerns: What are some of the key issues that affect this element of an orchestrated marketing program?

Analysis

SECTION PROFILE

Marketing Role

    Identify client wants/needs
    Identify program/service deficiencies
    Reduce the number of assumptions in setting strategies

Instruments

    Internal audit
    External audit of forces affecting marketplace
    User/nonuser characteristics, wants and needs
    Data interpretation/market segmentation
    Presentation of findings
    Assignment of implementation responsibilities
    Evaluation

Techniques

    Review of existing documents
    Surveys
    Numerical/nonnumerical interpretation

Conductor's Concerns

Is the information relevant and valid for determining the clients' desired benefits?

Is the information collected in a cost-effective manner?

Is the information properly arrayed for effective use and dissemination?

ANALYSIS

Knowledge is power. Nowhere is that adage truer than in marketing. Without adequate knowledge of the market environment and of the needs and perceptions of your users and potential users, the development of products to satisfy your clients will be left to intuition and professional judgment. Professional judgment certainly plays a key role in any successful marketing program, but basing services on the administrator's best guess can lead to serious problems.

In an orchestrated marketing program, Analysis is the foundation on which the rest of the process is built. Analysis entails both the collection and interpretation of data.

DATA COLLECTION

The first step in a market analysis is to gather the information to answer the question, "Where are we now?" The answer serves to describe the current marketing situation. It forms the baseline from which to speculate about the relevant future and to analyze the agency's marketing performance and potential. The methods for obtaining this baseline data involve:

 Internal audit

 External audit

 User/potential user analysis

Audit/analysis prelude. The information from these audits and analyses produces a comprehensive profile of the agency's total marketing effort and provides a basis for developing and revising a strategic marketing plan. For the purposes of this handbook, the terms "audit" and "analysis" will be used interchangeably. Before proceeding with the audits/analyses, three important and related decisions need to be made concerning the scope, data collection, methodology, and overall responsibility (auditor) of the audit.

Each audit should be comprehensive, but it should be limited to relevant inquiry, and it should reflect the agency's ability to use the information. Conducting an audit can take a considerable amount of effort, and each recreation and park organization must decide how detailed its audit should be and the amount of resources to commit to it. For example, small agencies may lack the resources to both collect detailed information and implement a large number of relatively detailed suggestions which may emerge. Hence, it may be most useful for such agencies to conduct a limited audit, concentrating on a relatively small number of selected items which are considered most critical.

The information needed to do the audit comes from three main sources: internal interviews, external interviews, and secondary documentary sources. Together, these three sources of information offer a broad-based approach for deriving an assessment of the agency's current marketing operations. The information which will be needed for evaluation should be identified at the beginning, and a mechanism should be established to make sure it is gathered in the form desired. Without this, the availability of certain kinds of information can tend to skew the audit itself.

Objectivity is an issue surrounding audits/analyses. Marketing audits may be conducted by someone from either within or outside of the agency. Be aware that self-audits often lack the objectivity of audits by outside persons or organizations and almost always carry less weight with decisionmakers.

<u>Internal audit</u>. The internal audit should be designed to take stock of the things your organization does and how well it does them from the viewpoint of the organization staff. The information will give you a baseline for making changes in your operations. The internal audit may take the form of a list of objective and subjective questions:

1. What do you do? (objective)

    a. What clients do you want to serve?

    b. What clients actually use your services?

    c. What services/facilities do you provide?

    d. Where and when are your services offered/facilities located?

    e. What do you charge for your services?

f. How do you promote your services?

   g. How do you analyze your market, users, nonusers?

   h. How do you evaluate the effectiveness of your services/facilities?

   i. Is your budget increasing? Decreasing?

2. How do you rate your effectiveness? (subjective)

   a. How well do you satisfy your clients' wants?

   b. Why do some potential clients avoid your services/facilities?

   c. What aspects of your marketing program need improvement?

A comprehensive list of questions may be found in Appendix 1.

The internal audit is the easiest part of the market analysis because the objective "What do we do?" questions can usually be answered by reference to existing documents, by observation, or by personal knowledge. The subjective self-appraisal part of the internal audit can be done through staff questionnaires, surveys, or interviews.

In San Jose, California, the Park and Recreation Department conducted a "Staff and Management Assessment" as one section of a four-part needs assessment process. The idea was to correlate staff perceptions with user perceptions and with objective maintenance quality analysis. The results was a recommended list of programs and services needing additional resources and a list of issues needing further study. Key to the process was a series of internal interviews with key individuals in the agency seeking to draw upon their knowledge of all aspects of the agency's operations, competencies, and constraints.

As part of the internal audit, an organization should also consider conducting interviews with key members of the organization's publics. Elected officials, suppliers, competitors, and customers should be asked for their impressions of how the organization is doing.

External audit. The internal audit should be supplemented by an analysis of the broader marketplace. This external audit is designed to provide your staff with a sense of where their organization fits within the overall recreation marketplace as well as the marketing opportunities that exist there. Part of the external audit is an analysis of other similar service providers and an assessment of the physical, social, and economic environment of the broad community your organization serves, your organizational history, and how information reaches the people you serve.

Too often, very little is known about the other agencies and organizations that provide services which are similar to yours. In client-oriented marketing, it is crucial to gain an understanding of what other providers are offering and how they deliver their programs. This understanding will enable your organization to determine an appropriate role for itself in the recreation marketplace and also will reveal some ideas you can adopt.

Recently, as a result of fiscal compression, many agencies have begun to reassess the feasibility of providing a full-service program. Some organizations are finding, as did the city of Campbell, California, that other providers can do a better job in providing certain programs, in this instance, instructional swim programs. This kind of decision can only be made with a knowledge of who else provides a service, coupled with an honest appraisal of your own agency's capabilities versus those of your competitors. In this way, the external and internal audits directly complement one another.

A successful organization has a "position" in the marketplace. This means that the organization has achieved a readily identifiable image with its clients that it provides certain services with a certain degree of quality. The McDonald's fast-food chain, for example, is one organization that has successfully established a position. Through an awareness of other providers, an organization can better ascertain its own position.

The process of analyzing other service providers begins with an inventory. Staff knowledge and a little time with the Yellow Pages and local newspapers can provide a suitable listing of the other providers. To analyze them, some of the same questions which you asked about your own organization in the internal audit should be asked about other providers. The answers will come from the promotional materials of these other service providers plus the observations of your staff. (See "External Audit" questions in Appendix 1.)

There is no mystery to the process of collecting information on the physical, social, and economic characteristics of your service area. Planning agencies, the U.S. Bureau of the Census, bank reports, local universities, and business bureaus all have valuable information that can help an organization map the location of physical features, commercial amenities (shopping centers, office complexes, industrial parks), identify transportation modes and patterns, and distinguish specific socioeconomic communities. An examination of the history of your service area sometimes yields information on significant events and personalities of the area. This may be useful in suggesting programs and promotional ideas.

Your external audit should also identify the information outlets that exist in your service area. All the newspapers, radio stations, outdoor advertising, community bulletin boards, and public relations firms should be inventoried and cross-referenced by audience reached.

Much of the information sought in the external audit is known by various staff in your organization. Many organizations find it valuable to take the time to write the information up in a form that can be referred to in developing marketing strategies. The external audit is, in fact, one of the important preludes to strategy development.

User/potential user analysis. An old marketing adage goes, "To sell Jack Jones what Jack Jones buys, you must see Jack Jones through Jack Jones' eyes." The single most important part of the market analysis process is the analysis of your users and potential users. Through this analysis, you will be able to see what your clientele wants and needs. Without this analysis, effective marketing is simply impossible. The following questions must be answered:

1. Users (your present clients)

   a. How often do your clients use your services/facilities?

   b. What benefits do they seek in using your services/facilities?

   c. How well are their expectations met?

   d. What are they willing to pay?

   e. How far and in what manner do they travel to reach your services/facilities?

       f. Where do they get their information on recreation opportunities?

       g. Where else do they go for services?

  2. Potential users (those nonusers who may want to participate?

       a. Who are they (demographics)?

       b. Why don't they use your services/facilities? (Transportation barriers? Price barriers? Lack of awareness? Disinterested?)

       c. What benefits are sought in a recreation experience?

       d. Where do they get their information on recreation opportunities?

Appendix 1 provides a more complete list of questions.

Survey research is the most accurate way to truly understand your users and potential users. Surveys cost money but there are ways to cut costs significantly. Many community planning agencies routinely conduct citizen surveys on a variety of issues, including recreation. Public recreation practitioners can work with the survey designers to include questions that will provide needed answers. Joint public/nonprofit/private recreation needs surveying is a distinct possibility that deserves consideration. Volunteers can certainly be used. In Scottsdale, Arizona, local college students not only conducted a user survey, they designed the questionnaire as well. The Parks and Recreation Department of Kettering, Ohio, utilized a university student volunteer to administer a citizen's survey form that had been prepared by another agency. Communities across the country have embraced the concept of citizen participation and utilize an arsenal of feedback mechanisms, including surveying, "hotlines," observation, town meetings, and one-to-one or small group dialogues.

Austin, Texas, like a number of other cities around the nation, recently undertook an extensive needs assessment as part of the Department of the Interior's Urban Park and Recreation Recovery Program. The assessment consisted of community meetings, on-site and door-to-door surveys, and quantitative analysis of service distribution. The assessment cost $120,000, a seemingly large sum. But at a cost of less than 30¢ per resident, the Austin Recreation and Parks Department obtained extremely accurate information on which to base its future directions. This information, put to use, could save the department a great deal by avoiding costly errors in programming, capital improvement, and site selection.

Marketing begins and ends with your clients. Their needs determine your programs, not the reverse. For this reason, the analysis of users and potential users is at the heart of effective marketing.

INTERPRETATION

Trends. The data collection step of market analysis is of paramount importance. Valid and reliable data provide the foundation on which market strategy decisions are made. All of the market analysis information gathered by an organization needs to be interpreted in the context of rapid change in four highly dynamic areas: economic trends, social trends, government trends, and technological trends.

Today's economic situation will change. Today's demographic balance is not tomorrow's. Government policies can change very quickly. New leisure products are constantly appearing. The direction of change should be carefully monitored by everyone in your organization.

Segmentation. Recreation marketing expert John Crompton recounts a story that illustrates an important marketing principle. A commercial rafting company running float trips on the Rio Grande River in Texas ran into a problem that occurs in many park settings. One trip in particular proved to be a disaster. Half the customers signed up and paid their money looking forward to a boisterous, beer drinking, good time on the river. The other half arrived expecting a contemplative tranquil experience. These differences in expectations quickly collided, and no one was satisfied with the trip. As this story illustrates, you can't expect one program to meet the needs of all clients. In order to serve your clients' particular needs, it is necessary to break down your total clientele into market segments with similar habits, preferences, and attitudes. The segmentation of your broad market is one of the key results of the market analysis.

Segmentation can be done in a number of ways. The most basic type of segmentation is geographic. Residents of a particular

community, for example, comprise a geographic segment about whom some conclusions can be drawn that will help in developing programs, services, and facilities to meet their needs. Most members of a geographic segment will tend to concentrate their shopping and their recreation time in certain areas. For this reason, the prime utility of geographic segmentation is in service or facility location. The major limitation of geographic segmentation is that it does not, by itself, distinguish demographic segments, which are more reliable indicators of similar behavior.

Demographic segmentation includes the identification of the traditional social categories, the most useful of which are age, sex, race, income, education, and family status. Usually, these segments are combined for greater predictive accuracy. For example, distinguishing men from women is usually necessary. But analyzing "men, 18-34," or "Hispanic men, 18-34," gives a much more precise basis for discerning behavior, attitudes, and preferences.

Despite wide variations in behavior within demographic segments, they are reasonably accurate predictors. As any parent knows, teenagers are remarkably similar in behavior, and most teenagers differ greatly in behavior and preferences from senior citizens. This is the value of demographic segmentation: many valuable predictions can be made about a market which has been demographically segmented.

Some marketers refine geographic and demographic segments into psychographic segments. Psychographic segmentation recognizes that in a marketplace with a broad range of choice available to the consumer, it is often necessary to develop products and services for segments that are more homogenous than even well-defined demographic segments. In psychographic segmentation, a market analyst looks for a recognizable "lifestyle," personality, or other intangible difference that will distinguish, for example, a 30-year-old female university professor earning $30,000 per year from a 30-year-old female carpenter also earning $30,000 per year. Psychographic segmentation permits the closest possible identification of client needs.

The "City Fit" program created in New Rochelle, New York, exemplifies the concept of market segmentation. Twelve sub-populations were identified as worthy targets for fitness programs. These represented the groups in New Rochelle which could benefit most from fitness programs.

Each market segment was viewed as a separate consumer group, and programs were tailored to accommodate the characteristics and idiosyncrasies of that group. Recreation, sports, and exercises were developed to meet the needs of each of these different populations. Equipment, time of day, location, and language were also considered. For example, the recreation department installed several pieces of specialized, fixed exercise equipment for use in the senior citizen centers.

A decision was also made to take the program to the people. One of the program's strengths was its acknowledgment of the population pluralism that characterized its community. In short, the community took a positive approach to developing, promoting, and delivering customized programs to many diverse market segments.

Geographic and demographic segmentation can be readily accomplished using information available through your local planning department or the U.S. Bureau of the Census. Psychographic segmentation requires the advice of social scientists and the use of user/potential user analysis information. A graduate student in psychology, sociology, or political science might be enlisted to help in psychographic segmentation of your broad market as a class project. Appendix 2 summarizes some of the prominent segmentation variables and typical breakdowns of each.

STRENGTHS, WEAKNESSES, AND OPPORTUNITIES

Interpretation of the data collected should provide a profile that identifies not only existing weaknesses and inhibiting factors but also the agency's strengths and new opportunities available to it. This is the summation of the data and constitutes a framework for adjusting the direction of your agency's programs.

POST-AUDIT/ANALYSIS TASKS

After the audit/analysis has been completed, four tasks remain to be done in order to ensure that full benefits accrue from the process.

First, when the information has been assembled its usefulness will depend upon the skill of the auditor in interpreting and successfully presenting it in a form in which the major points can quickly be grasped by decisionmakers. The presentation should address the overall performance of marketing operations. Recommendations have to be judged so that those which can contribute most to improving marketing performance are implemented first.

The second task is to ensure that the role of the audit has been clearly communicated and that the staff do not have higher expectations than the audit can realize. It is unlikely that suggestions will emerge that require radical changes in the way the agency operates. Its main role is to address the question, "Where are we now?" and to make some tentative suggestions about ways of improving what the organization already does.

The third post-audit task is to make someone accountable for ensuring that recommendations are implemented. We are all familiar with reports that have been prepared, presented, applauded, and filed away to gather dust. The person made accountable should be someone committed to the project, and someone who has the political clout and leverage to make things happen.

Finally, an agency should consider an appropriate interval between audits. It is recommended that this agency-wide audit should be undertaken every three to five years. A major commitment of resources is required to do it, so it is unrealistic to expect audits to be done more frequently. Although the initial cost as measured by effort and resource expenditure may appear high, like many new tasks, it is likely to be less costly when the process is repeated.

The marketing audit process is complemented by ongoing evaluations of the relative success or failure of selected agency programs. This process is termed program evaluation. Program evaluations provide early warning signals that a program is not adequately meeting the needs and desires of its targeted clientele. Program evaluation is concerned with evaluation of the individual program, in contrast to the marketing audit which focuses on evaluation of the total set of agency programs. Conceptually, the marketing audit emerges from a summation, synthesis, and integration of the annual evaluations of each program.

Strategy Development

SECTION PROFILE

<u>Marketing Role</u>

    Select target market segments based on consumer wants and agency objectives
    Select a mix of strategies to produce the best results

<u>Instruments</u>

    Goal setting
    Targeting
    Strategy mix
      Product
      Price
      Promotion
      Distribution

<u>Techniques</u>

    Reference to market analysis
    Research specific comparables

<u>Conductor's Concerns</u>

    Will the program address the problems identified in the analysis?

    How feasible is the strategy for the organization and for the market environment?

    Can the objectives and strategies be quantified for evaluation?

    How flexible is the strategy for unanticipated developments?

STRATEGY DEVELOPMENT

After you've analyzed the marketplace, your organization's performance and position, the needs and perceptions of your users and potential users, and after segmenting the broad market into useful groupings, your organization is ready to move into market strategy development.

Market strategy development culminates in an implementation (action) plan which guides the realignment of the organization's resources toward satisfying the clients' needs. It involves three steps:

    Goal setting

    Selection of target market segments

    Designing the strategy mix

GOAL SETTING

Apart from the daily challenges of "putting out brush fires," nearly all organizations work from an identified list of objectives. For an organization adopting an orchestrated marketing approach, these objectives should relate directly to the client needs identified in the market analysis phase. Goals should be based on an in-depth evaluation and interpretation of the data collected during the market analysis.

Setting goals for your marketing program brings you back to a key question: "What business are you in?" Your marketing goals must help you accomplish the mission of your agency. The park and recreation organization which presumes it is in the youth sports or tennis or swimming or arts and crafts business is viewing its mission from a product rather than a client service orientation. A recreation agency may be in business to enhance community physical and mental health, facilitate the learning of pleasurable and useful skills, provide services to special needs populations, or bring about neighborhood identity and pride. These are client-service-related missions. If financial self-sufficiency, equal service to disabled residents, service to all regardless of ability to pay, or cooperation with other agencies are policies of your organization, then your marketing goals must conform to those policies, as well as accomplish your organization's mission.

Your marketing goals should meet two prime criteria: they should be specific and measurable. Typical long-term (three years plus) marketing goals for a public recreation agency might include:

1. Increase awareness of selected programs among teenage boys by 20 percent

2. Increase family participation in selected programs by 15 percent

3. Develop three joint programs with the local military installation to serve both military dependents and the general community

4. Provide services to 1,000 disabled residents

Marketing goals, like any other goals, should be realistic. No organization should develop a list of marketing objectives that is too extensive or too difficult to accomplish. It's better to achieve challenging but realistic goals than fall short on unrealistic goals.

Occasionally, various goals and policies will be contradictory; managers should urge policy makers to eliminate the contradictions or at least arrange goals in order of priority. Resolution of conflicts will be greatly simplified.

TARGETING

Long-term goals do not generally specify particular programs or services to be provided. Specific services are identified through short-term objectives. Both long-term and short-term objectives suggest client groups to be served, called target market segments. Targeting flows logically from goal setting.

Selection of target market segments is one of the more important choices an organization will make and is crucial in designing an effective market strategy. Even an organization with a broad mission, like the YMCA, can't serve all of the hundreds of possible market segments. With limited resources and limited expertise, choices must be made. A choice to serve one market segment is a choice not to serve another. The selection of target market segments helps determine an organization's position in the marketplace. It can also bring about efficiency by leaving service of some market segments to other organizations better equipped or staffed to serve them.

DESIGNING A STRATEGY MIX

As already emphasized, the most effective market strategies are those that are custom designed to satisfy the needs of the market segments your organization has targeted for service. If this were not the case, it would be a simple matter to develop a market strategy on the "one size fits all" principle. As it is, with each target market segment having a unique set of needs and seeking a unique set of benefits, strategy development becomes creative artistry.

A marketing strategy consists of a blending of four factors: product, price, promotion, and distribution. A marketer's skill lies in striking the right note in these four components to produce a harmonious sound. This is artistry, indeed, since a small change in any one of the strategy components will change the sound of the chord produced and will change the appeal of its sound to a given target market.

PRODUCT

Product refers to the services, programs, facilities, or items offered by your organization to your target market segments. Product is the prime vehicle through which your organization meets, or fails to meet, the needs of its clients. The market analysis, especially the user/potential user analysis, should provide you with pertinent information on the values, needs, and benefits your target market segments want in recreation products, as well as a sense of the preferred products themselves.

A product is not simply the basic offering--a dance class, for example. It's a jazz dance class or a square dance class with child care provided, or a dance class with a T-shirt for each participant. The product, then, can be designed with countless variations to the basic offering. Each variation responds to the identified needs of distinct target segments.

In Minneapolis, the YMCA targeted a fitness class for middle-age women. With a young woman as the instructor, participation was less than expected. But with a middle-age woman as instructor, the class became one of the Y's most popular offerings. A change in one feature, the instructor, changed the receptivity of the target market segment.

For many hard-to-reach target market segments, the staffing feature is the key to product success. The most successful youth gang diversion programs in cities from Philadelphia to San Jose employ streetworkers with racial and ethnic backgrounds similar to those of the young clients. Selection of the staff is done in response to the needs of the target market segment.

Consider, too, the physical attributes of your facilities. Do they satisfy the expectations of your target market segments? Are they clean and comfortable enough? Cleanliness is a prime product attribute for many target market segments. A poorly maintained restroom can counteract an entire day's enjoyment for many people. By the same token orderliness by itself can be a turnoff for some target markets. Kids often feel more at home with a degree of disorder than in a highly structured environment that they may perceive as antiseptic.

It all depends on the point of view of the market segment in question. Products should always be designed with that point of view in mind. If your products are relevant to the wants and needs of your target market, they may succeed. Their success is also dependent on other factors of market strategy. But if products are not relevant to the needs of the clientele, no other marketing magic can rescue them and they are destined to fail.

PRICE

Price is another marketing strategy variable. There was a time when pricing was to many public and nonprofit recreation agencies as rock and roll was to dedicated classical music fans...incomprehensible. But even as many symphony orchestras are offering "pops" programs and featuring rock musicians as soloists, so pricing is today very much a part of the marketing strategy of all recreation organizations--public, nonprofit, and private.

Just as products must be designed to meet the needs of specific client groups, pricing must be custom-tailored for specific target markets. What is the right price to charge and what will be the practical effect of pricing decisions? These are key questions.

Often the primary goal in setting a price is return on investment and revenue generation. But price has other purposes as well: maintaining or improving an image; adding services; instilling a sense of product value; controlling misuse; and assuring equity in service distribution. All of these goals can be at least as important as strictly financial objectives.

The decision not to impose a cost on a service is certainly a pricing decision. Some organizations have established traditions of free or low-cost service and thus make pricing decisions in order to maintain that tradition. A classic example of the reverse phenomenon was the inspired decision by the Hanes hosiery company several years ago to double the price of its pantyhose. This was purely a pricing decision; it was based on no change in the quality of the hose. The effect was an immediate perception on the part of the consumers that Hanes was a better product than its virtually identical competitors. Within months, Hanes had doubled its market share and had changed the thinking of an entire industry.

The Hanes example relates closely to another pricing feature: the relationship between price and perceived quality. Many people believe that "you get what you pay for." Most of us attach a higher value to something we've paid a lot of money for than something that was low cost or free. This positive relationship between price and value is established early in life. The small child will value the kitten she's paid 25¢ for more than the free kitten. Pricing, then, can serve to strengthen participant loyalty. Recognizing the price/value relationship is very important in marketing. Often, instead of turning off a target segment, a charge will automatically make a particular service just that much more enjoyable or meaningful.

Equally important is the recognition that fees create a responsibility on the part of the organization charging them. While an increase in cost intrinsically increases the perceived value of a service, a price increase also raises consumer expectations. Pricing decisions should reflect awareness that increased fees create increased expectations. If an organization is not able to maintain and enhance the quality of a service, it should reconsider the wisdom of imposing or raising a fee.

PEOPLE OFTEN ATTACH A HIGHER VALUE TO SOMETHING FOR WHICH THEY PAY THAN SOMETHING THEY GET FOR FREE.

Quite a few public recreation agencies have included revenue-generating features to free or low-cost recreation destinations. Highly profitable "amusement centers" are routinely designed into or retrofitted onto swimming pools, lakes, and other primary attractions. A number of marketing goals are accomplished through this vehicle. For example, features are added to a product, additional services are provided, revenues are produced, promotional potential is enhanced, and the needs of several market segments satisfied.

Pricing decisions can change usership in some subtle and striking ways. Some of these changes can be anticipated; others cannot. In California, the Hayward Area Recreation and Park District raised golfing fees and discovered that the increase caused a drastic drop in attendance by senior citizens, defeating both revenue and service goals. Adjusting fees downward during nonpeak use hours mid-week restored much of the usership, which allowed the district to increase its weekend revenue. The initial decision to raise prices was a marketing decision that backfired because the agency miscalculated certain clients' ability and willingness to pay. A more complete analysis may have prevented the temporary estrangement of the senior golfers.

In Sacramento County, California, the park department encountered strong resistance to a new fee. In one episode, the entry gates to a county park were burned down. The county realized that the problem would best be dealt with through a campaign explaining the necessity of charging fees. Experience has shown that there is a predictable period of resistance to the imposition of a fee at a formerly free facility. If an agency properly prepares the clientele for a price imposition or increase through a prepublicity campaign, within a few months, usership should build back up to former levels.

The San Jose Recreation and Park Department used fees to change usership at one troubled facility. This facility was designed for family use, but the presence of motorcycle gangs and car clubs effectively deterred other users. A minimal parking fee was enough to dissuade gang and car club members from using the park, permitting a return of family users.

The right price to charge for a product is based on organization objectives coupled with the ability and willingness of users to pay. Revenue generation is an objective of most public and nonprofit recreation organizations. Service to all, regardless of ability to pay,

may be another objective that affects pricing decisions.
Providing services that do not put commercial recreation
providers out of business may be another objective affecting
pricing decisions.

Ability to pay for recreation services needs to be thoroughly
assessed in pricing decisions. With a trend toward less
disposable personal income, increasing numbers of recreation
users will be forced to carefully weigh a choice to purchase
a recreation service against a purchase of some other more
immediate need--clothing, food, or transportation, for example.
At the same time, most people accept the notion of fees for
public services and are willing to pay. Again, the market
segments you target for service and the policies of your
organization and political jurisdiction dictate the feasibility of imposing a charge or will suggest how high the
charge should be. The <u>Fees and Charges Handbook</u>, available
from the National Park Service, describes some methods for
overcoming the exclusionary effects of service fees.

The city of Weston, Massachusetts, employs a once-a-year
"all-inclusive" fee system with great success. An annual
fee of $35 entitles an entire family to free access to all
facilities and programs administered by the Parks and
Recreation Department. Each May, applications for the passes
are processed by part-time student employees and mailed back
to the families. Sixty percent of the city's residents
take advantage of this system and revenues from user fees
have risen from $12,000 to $70,000 annually since the system
was instituted. Overhead was drastically cut since money
transactions at facilities are now minimal.

Prices for recreation services can be based directly on the
cost of providing the service or established in some other
way. Cost-based pricing methods are the following:

1. Variable cost pricing in which the price covers all
   variable costs but no fixed costs

2. Partial overhead pricing in which the price covers
   all variable costs and some fixed costs

3. Average cost pricing in which the price covers
   all fixed and variable costs

Fixed costs are those which do not vary with the number of
participants. Variable costs are those related to the
number of participants. Variable cost pricing is the most

popular cost-based pricing method used by public recreation providers because it permits lower costs. It assumes that the fixed costs should be publicly paid since public recreation potentially benefits all residents, users and non-users. With a reduction in tax-generated revenues, public recreation agencies have begun to explore cost-based pricing that recovers more of the total cost of services.

There are two noncost-based pricing methodologies: going-rate pricing and demand-oriented pricing.

Going-rate pricing is popular because it is easily established and does not "undercut" other service providers if the other service providers used for comparison include a range from the public, nonprofit, and private sectors. A drawback to this pricing method is that the going rate may be irrational, out-of-date, too high, or too low.

Demand-oriented pricing establishes prices based on the ability/willingness of client groups to pay for a particular service. It results in different prices for different client groups, similar facilities in different locations, different places within a facility (i.e. orchestra versus balcony seats), or different times. The keys to successful demand-oriented pricing is acceptance by all clients of the validity of the pricing differentials and lack of stigma on those paying a lower price.

PROMOTION

Promotion is the third ingredient of the marketing mix and the one with which agencies have the most experience. Promotion is communication; it is the process by which your well-designed and properly priced products are brought to the attention of your target market segments.

The best promotion strategy is one which employs a number of techniques. The properly balanced combination is called the "promotional mix" and is made up of publicity, advertising, personal contact, and special promotions.

Publicity. The process of getting your newsworthy items reported in the media is publicity. Newsworthy stories are determined by the media, not the organization seeking publicity. Remember that the media exist to sell advertising, and their success is measured by the number of readers, listeners, and viewers. The CBS television program

"60 Minutes," one of the most popular offerings in the media, sells its advertising space at the rate of over $260,000 per minute, which is two to three times more than the rate for other programs with a viewership one-half to one-third as large. Your information, then, is useful to the media to the extent that it helps to retain and/or expand an audience.

Experienced marketers get to know media people, particularly those responsible for reporting on the activities of their organizations. They develop a "sixth sense" of what information works best for each particular media contact, and how they can make their contacts' work easier. In Dade County, Florida, the recreation department public information officer hand delivers press releases to the appropriate newspaper editor. The East Bay Regional Park District in Oakland, California, films and photographs special events and distributes the films and photos to television networks unable to attend the event.

Besides the commercial media, newsletters, brochures, information booths, and on-site staff information services are publicity devices, and are used by most recreation organizations.

Publicity is excellent promotion, but it is highly unpredictable. Your most exciting event of the year may get bumped from the front page or prime time coverage it deserves by other local, national, or international events. In addition, you have very little control over which particular medium chooses to provide publicity. This makes publicity less targetable than other kinds of promotion.

Advertising. Offering many of the same features as publicity, advertising, in addition, is more controllable. Also, it usually costs more than publicity. Its main purpose is to create and reinforce an image over a long period. The advertiser is concerned most with providing information to a large but specific audience by such methods as direct mail and outdoor advertising, as well as the better known "paid for" spots in the print and electronic media.

The primary consideration in advertising is the "reach" of the medium. Reach defines the volume, type, and geographic spread of the audience. Other important advertising terms/considerations are:

    1. Frequency--the number of times an advertising message reaches its audience

2. Delivery--the place or situation in which the message is received

3. Selectivity--the ability to target specific market segments

These considerations are points of comparison in determining the overall effectiveness of alternative advertising channels. Because advertising will usually cost you money, it pays to thoroughly research advertising alternatives before you buy.

Advertising costs are usually calculated by cost per thousand people reached. Television, for example, is the most expensive, but generally it has a low cost per thousand reached. The relatively low cost per thousand reached also reflects a relatively untargeted effect versus newspapers or radio which can be more precisely targeted.

Public agencies and nonprofit recreation organizations throughout the country receive free advertising on radio, television, and outdoor billboards donated as a public service. Each June, the <u>Miami Herald</u> donates an entire page of advertising space to the public recreation agency in Dade County. Promotion of recreation programs in Natick, Massachusetts, costs the taxpayers very little. Local merchants sponsor ads which pay the cost of producing the town's recreation program brochures. The merchants also distribute the brochures in their places of business. The brochures are distributed to all students (grades 1-12) at school through a cooperative arrangement with local public school officials.

In Newport Beach, California, the Department of Parks, Beaches, and the Arts borrowed an idea from nearby Anaheim and turned over production and distribution of its program brochure to a private advertising firm. In return for revenues from advertising space, the firm designs, prints, and distributes a brochure of superior quality at no cost to the city. The city retains quality control through absolute veto power on the nature, content, and amount of advertising.

Public service billboards are often available for the asking during certain slack periods in the outdoor advertising cycle. The "Friends of the Zoo" in San Francisco received $30,000 worth of billboard space from a large outdoor advertising firm. As a public service, the "Friends" were given use of dozens of billboards for a one-year period. The free advertising for the Adopt-An-Animal program resulted in over $100,000 in new memberships.

Negotiation is often utilized in the advertising business. Suggest to advertising representatives that your organization would like to try out their channel free or at a reduced rate with the possibility of future commissions. Don't be shy. Remember that unless you ask, your chances of getting donated advertising are slim.

The key to advertising, as with all promotional tools, is targeting for impact on selected target markets. An upcoming National Park Service publication on promotion will provide many helpful suggestions for getting the most from your advertising dollar.

<u>Personal contact.</u> Activities often referred to as customer relations or direct contact are known as personal contact. Promotional activities of this kind involve your entire staff working with the client. This type of interaction provides your clients with a positive experience, and its importance cannot be overemphasized. This kind of experience creates good word-of-mouth promotion, the kind that money can't buy. Staff training on policies, procedures, hospitality, and basic interpersonal communication fosters successful customer relations and results in positive user experience. Agencies are well advised to commit some resources to staff development in this important area.

Customer relations sometimes involves a form of personal selling. Personal selling might include speaker bureaus, information desks/booths/windows, on-site staff information services, complaint phone lines, and customer suggestion boxes. Indirectly, advisory boards, town meetings, commission meetings, and needs assessment activities all enhance your customers' attitude toward your agency and its services and may therefore be considered customer relations.

Through personal contact, a staff member of your organization works with a limited number of targeted individuals or groups. The purpose of the contact may be to make the target market segment aware of your services, to solicit their participation, or both. Fund-raising contacts are also of this type of promotion. So, too, are efforts to inform leisure counselors or commercial businesses of your activities in order that they may be suggested to community visitors. School groups, social and civic clubs, and employee associations all constitute made-to-order blocks of business which can be contacted directly. Many commercial theme parks attribute up to 30 percent of their total attendance to these publics. How about creating an army of direct contact promoters of your services?

In Needham, Massachusetts, the Park and Recreation Department utilizes a "consumers as recruiters" concept. Strong program supporters are encouraged to recruit others, particularly in programs which need a minimum number of participants. Staff program leaders also actively recruit users through direct solicitation.

Special promotions. This last method, special promotions, draws heavily on the other three methods of promotion. They are often used to encourage use of a new product or stimulate use of an old one. Special promotion tools include incentives, contests or games, special events, and joint promotional campaigns.

Incentives can provide that extra infusion of "value" which attracts the user. Introductory offers are popular and they work. To help celebrate and simultaneously promote the opening of a women's fitness center at a YMCA in San Francisco, a special discount membership rate was offered.

Special off-season and off-hour prices and free samples are other examples of incentives. T-shirts are excellent incentive premiums. People love them and they can be designed for effective advertising.

Care should be taken to avoid cheapening the experience or creating misleading expectations in the mind of the user. "Price-off" incentives should not be construed as being permanent.

Contests and games can help promote a product or service, but they require an understanding of applicable legal requirements and restrictions. People are strongly drawn to contests by an innate urge to "take a chance." It is important that the contest have a thematic relationship to the product or service it is helping to promote.

Special events not only promote awareness of facilities and services, they also stimulate high one-time use. They are excellent promotions because they set the organization apart from other similar service providers. Ideally, the initial uniqueness established through a special event will remain with those who attended and translate into long-term patronage.

Sometimes, there is an overwhelming impact from a special event. Gilroy, California, expected 3,000 people when it held its first Garlic Festival in 1978. More than 30,000 showed up. In 1981, the crowd soared to more than 100,000 during the weekend period. And in 1982, paid attendance was up six percent from last year, netting over $250,000. The festival has quickly become the town's largest moneymaker in the category of special events, with over $100,000 in revenues benefiting Gilroy community organizations.

In North Conway, New Hampshire, the Park and Recreation Department created an event known as the "Mud Bowl" in which several New England teams compete in a very muddy (18-inch deep) football game. In 1980, the Miller Brewing Co. provided $7,000 in free advertising, and the event raised $5,000, which was channeled through a nonprofit recreation organization for recreation programs. The concept has since spread to communities in upstate New York.

Joint promotion, or "cross promotion" as it is called in the marketing trade, is an excellent way to cut promotional costs. Through this device, two or more organizations combine forces to benefit one another.

For example, in La Habra, California, the Park and Recreation Department worked with the local McDonald's franchise in promoting a resident survey. The department sent out survey forms to community residents with an offer of a free beverage at McDonald's with each returned form. McDonald's helped the department by offering an incentive to fill out the forms, and the department offered McDonald's an incentive for gaining new customers, who more often than not purchased food to go with their drink.

In Peabody, Massachusetts, the Bell Corporation sponsors special events and earmarks a portion of the price of Burger King hamburgers for the purchase of recreation equipment, which is turned over to the Parks and Recreation Department. The Burger King outlets gain considerable publicity from their participation in this joint program.

In 1980, the San Francisco Park and Recreation Department teamed up with the Perrier Corporation and local businesses to turn the grand opening of a parcourse into a special event which raised $8,100 for park operations.

As a service to customers, many rental car agencies and tourist bureaus maintain racks of brochures describing things to do in the area. A park or recreation agency should use this form of joint promotion to help attrack users.

The sale of advertising space in recreation agency program booklets and the distribution of the booklets by advertisers is an increasingly common example of cross promotion. The phone company in Simi Valley, California, features a different city recreation facility on the cover of each new phone book it produces. This, too, is a form of cross promotion.

Public agencies have every reason to cooperate with each other on joint promotions. In Needham, Massachusetts, the public library, Council on Aging, school department, and the Youth Commission all promote the programs of the municipal recreation department through their publications. The recreation department reciprocates in their publications. This is a two-way exchange in that each agency assists the other in promoting programs for specific populations.

Umbrella marketing, a relatively new concept, is becoming valuable in view of rising advertising costs and increased competition for the public's attention. This type of promotion ties several products (facilities or programs) together, usually with a common theme. Most likely to gain from umbrella marketing are the less popular facilities and programs which don't normally justify large promotional efforts, but which are targeted for increased use. A new service might be promoted along with other, more familiar programs to entice new clients. The umbrella approach is being tried in some commercial ad campaigns. The best known is General Electric's "We Bring Good Things to Life" ads, which present as many as 13 products in a single 60-second television commercial. This entices buyers (clients) of one brand (service) to try another less familiar one.

Tourist bureaus commonly use umbrealla marketing to promote a large array of activities in pursuit of increased overall tourism. For an investment of less than $9 million, the state of New York increased its multimillion dollar tourist industry by 19 percent, in large part due to its successful "I Love New York" campaign.

The by-products of promotion are "image" and "identity." Image is the impression associated with your agency in the minds of those who are aware of your services. If your organization has a positive image of responsiveness, vibrancy, and efficiency--work hard to maintain it. Remember, first

IF YOUR ORGANIZATION HAS A POSITIVE IMAGE - - WORK HARD TO MAINTAIN IT

impressions, both favorable and unfavorable, are lasting. You'll work harder and spend more overcoming a negative image, whether or not its deserved, than maintaining a positive one. Identity refers to the instantaneous association of your services and products in the minds of your market. Identity is established by consistently maintaining quality products, logos, color themes uniforms, and enough exposure so that an immediate mental association occurs when someone sees one of your symbols of identity.

The specific promotional techniques you adopt and how they are phased will depend on the market segments you desire to serve. Your promotional mix should be calculated to make a specific segment aware of the benefits they will receive by using your product or service. Remember, you are promoting benefits, not services. You effectively promote your services by promoting the benefits of these services to perspective clients.

DISTRIBUTION

Distribution is the fourth marketing strategy concept. It addresses who gets what, when, where, and how. Central to distribution is the concept of equity, which directly relates to the agency's mission, marketing objectives, and target market selection. For most public agencies, equity is the accepted standard for the allocation of services, and it is the obligation to ensure equity that distinguishes public agencies from commercial enterprises.

While most distribution decisions result in the physical siting of a facility or service, there are a number of steps which lead up to location. These steps involve evaluating existing distribution patterns, establishing distribution objectives, determining whether the distribution will be direct or indirect, selecting the location, actually delivering the service, and monitoring the delivery.

Optimal distribution entails the correct siting of services and facilities to provide for target market segments. For correct siting to occur, the target client groups should be identified and the existing distribution pattern of the particular facility or service plotted. Service deficiencies should be easily identified. Subsequent facility and program sitings should occur in these deficient service locations.

The siting of services, particularly those that involve costly facilities, must bear careful consideration. In

these austere times, agencies are looking for locations
that don't involve a heavy capital commitment. Facility
sharing between school districts, public recreation agencies,
and nonprofit organizations can help all these entities
distribute their services in accordance with their respective
goals. Corporations are often willing to make their
facilities available, too. Fireman's Fund Insurance Company,
while headquartered in San Francisco, made its corporate
auditorium available to community groups and nonprofit
organizations.

Faced with the inability to increase the number of fixed
facilities, agencies often turn to innovative "outreach"
service delivery methods. The Detroit Park and Recreation
Department, along with the many others around the country,
has mobile facilities which permit precise location of
services for impact on selected market segments. To
compensate for an inequitable distribution of swimming
pools, the department will truck in small pools to some of
its clients. Mobile theaters, mobile arts and crafts,
mobile equipment vans--these are all distribution devices,
and many recreation organizations use them.

Outlets are distribution tools, too. For many kinds of
services and products, the best way to reach the intended
clients is to utilize outlets for distribution. Greenpeace,
a highly effective national environmental organization,
receives substantial support from the sale of a line of
products through outlets located in cities across the
country. These outlets constitute distribution channels.
Often, it is much more convenient for an agency's clients
to pick up a program brochure or purchase tickets to a
community theater production at the local record store than
at the offices of the agency. The increasing use of
computerized reservation and ticket services by the National
Park Service and many state parks departments is an example
of utilizing outlets to improve service distribution.

Outlets, in effect, represent indirect service distribution.
The effectiveness of an organization's distribution can
be enhanced through indirect distribution in a number of
ways. More and more, park and recreation agencies are
acting as facilitators, or brokers, for other public and
private providers. A number of these agencies are
redefining their roles from direct service delivery to
brokerage. This brokerage role means that the services are
provided by other individuals and organizations. The
agency is in business to see that needed services are
provided by someone, wherever and whenever they are needed.

When services are available is a make or break issue. In the Las Vegas area, softball leagues play around the clock serving the needs of casino shift workers and taking advantage of cooler night temperatures. Adult fitness programs achieve higher enrollments when offered at locations close to those primarily interested in such programs--working men and women--and at times which are convenient to them--lunchtime and immediately after work.

Distribution questions--what? where? when? who? and how?-- are marketing questions. Distribution must be viewed in light of clients' needs just as much as product, price, and promotion.

Implementation

SECTION PROFILE

<u>Marketing Role</u>

    Accomplish strategies selected
    Achieve established objectives

<u>Instruments</u>

    Gaining consensus
    Assigning responsibilities
    Leadership

<u>Techniques</u>

    Personal contact
    Group interaction
    Task forces/advisory groups
    Job descriptions
    Incentives

<u>Conductor's Concerns</u>

    Can staff/volunteer/decisionmaker consensus be obtained and maintained?

    Is there a process to insure task accomplishment?

    Are all implementation decisions at each phase of the marketing process adequately interrelated?

IMPLEMENTATION

By now, you will be well aware that marketing is a client service orientation for your agency or organization. As such, marketing is everyone's responsibility. The first step in implementation, therefore, must be to gain consensus among your organization staff and decisionmakers on the need for marketing.

GAINING CONSENSUS

Everyone in your organization, from board members to volunteers, should be given a chance to air their concerns, ask questions, and provide their own vision on marketing your agency or organization. Some staff members may initially balk at the concept of marketing. If people are hung up on the word "marketing," substitute a different word or phrase. How about "client service program"? That's really what it's all about.

RESPONSIBILITIES

Once staff, board, and volunteers have gained an understanding and appreciation for marketing, specific marketing tasks can be designed into their daily responsibilities. After all, each individual plays an important role in creating an image of quality and service and in delivering a first-rate product.

Maintenance workers do more than repair and maintain facilities. They are highly visible to park visitors and can serve as your front-line public relations representatives. Your designers and planners conduct market research and can take responsibility for converting research data into successful market strategies. Recreation instructors and interpretors help design your products and should have some responsibility in helping develop promotion strategies.

As prominent members of the community, your board or commission members can serve a major role in promoting your organization through personal contact and are in a good position to receive valuable community feedback on your organization's services.

Volunteers can assist in all aspects of marketing. Examples abound of students or youth group volunteers assisting on user surveys and direct solicitations. In Pasadena, California, volunteer board members of a nonprofit "Friends of Recreation" organization are the recreation department's best promoters. In Simi Valley, California, scout troops distributed recreation program announcements in return for free use of facilities.

Elected officials in your community also can play a marketing role. Public relations is an important part of their jobs, and they can usually benefit politically from assisting in promotion activities if scheduled well in advance. In Detroit, the mayor's office was instrumental in the production of a gifts catalog for the city.

To reinforce each staff member's marketing responsibilities, an organization should consider evaluating employees on their marketing performance. In San Jose, California, the Park and Recreation Department writes marketing responsibilities into employee job descriptions.

In assigning marketing tasks to staff members, an organization has an obligation to provide adequate training on important roles each staff member plays. The Miami, Florida, Parks and Recreation Department provides sensitivity training for staff who interact with disabled users. The YMCA organization in San Francisco holds quarterly retreats for staff in key public contact positions to discuss customer relations. As managers know, employees can do the job right only if given the right skills.

LEADERSHIP

An orchestra needs a dynamic and capable conductor in order to produce the most harmonious sound. An orchestrated marketing program requires leadership, particularly given the interrelationship between each component of a marketing program. Here are a few leadership options:

1. Most agencies or organizations assign the coordination of press relations or public information responsibilities to one individual or organizational unit.

2. Some agencies, like the Foothills Metropolitan Recreation and Park District in Lakewood, Colorado,

have taken a cue from the private sector and appointed the equivalent of a "director of marketing" to oversee all phases of marketing.

3. Some organizations have marketing committees composed of staff from all levels of the hierarchy. In San Francisco, a group made up of prominent representatives of the private sector and the general community are looking at ways to improve the marketing program of the city's recreation and park department.

Marketing professionals strongly advise that leadership is necessary to keep the sections of the marketing orchestra playing together and in harmony, and to make adjustments in the market strategy mix to produce the most well-promoted, -priced, and -distributed programs possible.

LEADERSHIP IS NECESSARY TO KEEP THE SECTIONS OF THE MARKETING ORCHESTRA PLAYING TOGETHER AND IN HARMONY.

Evaluation

SECTION PROFILE

<u>Marketing Role</u>

    Ascertain effectiveness of marketing strategies
    Determine reliability of analysis
    Evaluate the effectiveness of implementation measures

<u>Instruments</u>

    Quantitative analysis
    Qualitative analysis

<u>Techniques</u>

    Continuous and directed review
    Drawing conclusions

<u>Conductor's Concerns</u>

    Is the evaluation timely and responsive?

    Is objectivity being maintained?

    Is the feedback complete and unbiased?

    Can the evaluation be readily translated into program improvements?

EVALUATION

Let's return to the analogy of an orchestra. Without proper evaluation, the conductor and players will have very little idea of how well the performance is going, which instruments are off key, when the tempo is off, when the audience can't hear one of the instruments, or even the listeners are indifferent to the piece being played. When the audience's applause is thunderous, the orchestra knows it has done well. Less enthusiastic responses can be translated into evaluative information on which to make needed adjustments.

All organizations evaluate their programs in one way or another. The most typical way is through quantitative analysis, to focus on the numbers of participants or amount of revenue generated. The temptation is to equate high numbers with success. Numbers tell part of the story. If few people show up for a major event, you can assume something went wrong. But you need more qualitative feedback to really gauge the effectiveness of your marketing mix. You need to know not only how many people are participating, but also which segments are participating, are they participating on a repeat basis, and are they satisfied with the service they are getting.

The interrelationship between market analysis, strategy development, and evaluation should be obvious, especially in the interplay between market analysis information and the development of an effective strategy. Evaluation is an ongoing process of monitoring the success of actions undertaken in implementing your strategy.

Each market strategy component can be analyzed both quantitatively and qualitatively. Comparison of attendance and revenue figures against predetermined performance standards drawn from your records or from the performance of similar recreation service providers gives quantitative feedback. On-site interviews, suggestion boxes, or surveys allow opportunities for qualitative feedback. Promotion techniques can be tested through the use of redeemable coupons, or through carefully monitored participant/media promotion analysis. The use of "focus groups," five to ten people specially selected to represent a specific target market, can be very valuable in suggesting areas of your marketing program needing adjustment.

Your overall marketing program merits semiannual or quarterly evaluation. Progress toward reaching short- and long-term marketing objectives should be assessed and a new course charted if the old one is not fruitful.

Evaluation of individual products should be conducted at numerous phases of the product life cycle. In fact, evaluation measures and expectations (satisfaction, use, or revenue) should be engineered into the product. Whatever problems you discover through the evaluation process--attendance drop off, increase in complaints, increase in misuse--will suggest when it's time to conduct a major re-analysis of your market environment.

Self-evaluation is a valid and necessary process, but there is a need to watch objectivity. The use of objective performance measures and the input of an objective third party can lend reliability to the evaluation process. Perhaps your "Friends" organization could conduct or arrange a yearly major program analysis.

Evaluation is a reality check for your organization. It enables you to know what you're doing well and what you can do better. It's proof that you mean business when you describe your marketing program as a "client service orientation."

CODA

In music, a coda is a final passage that brings a piece to a close. In orchestrated marketing, Evaluation brings the process full circle, but not to a close. Marketing has no concluding note, no final downbeat. It is a continual thought process, prevailing attitude, and consistent approach geared to pleasing your audience and doing your job right.

We encourage you to make a critical appraisal of how well you are achieving your organizational and professional goals. We invite you to consider client-oriented marketing as an approach for your organization to adopt.

Appendices

APPENDIX 1

A MARKETING AUDIT OUTLINE

I. <u>INTERNAL AUDIT</u>

    A. What do you do?

        1. What is the mission of your agency? What business is it in? How well is its mission understood throughout the organization? What business does it wish to be in five years from now?

        2. What are the stated objectives of the organization? Are they formally written down? Do they lead logically to clearly stated marketing objectives?

        3. What policies inhibit the achievement of your objectives with respect to organization, allocation of resources, operations, hiring and training, products, pricing, and promotion?

        4. Who uses the agency's services?

        5. What are the major services offered by the agency? Do they complement each other, or is there unnecessary duplication?

        6. How are facility locations selected?

        7. When are services made available to users?

        8. How frequently are services offered? Are there multiple offerings?

        9. Is there a current written pricing policy statement?

       10. Are prices reviewed at least annually? Are price increases keeping pace with cost increases or general inflation levels?

       11. What mechanisms does the agency have to ensure that disadvantaged groups are not excluded from participating by prices charged?

12. Does the agency use price promotions effectively?

13. What are the procedures for establishing and reviewing pricing policy?

14. How are public relations normally handled by the agency? By whom?

15. Are there agency policies restricting some public relations activities?

16. What media are current being used for advertising?

17. How is promotion designed for and directed to different markets? Is it all the same, one universal approach?

18. How do users find out about and decide to try and/or use the organization's services? When and where?

19. How have agency personnel used the information which they have generated about the agency's markets and other publics to improve services?

20. Does the organization carry out periodic reviews of its programs and evaluations of its resource allocation decisions?

21. Does the organization have a marketing planning and evaluation system?

22. Are enough resources (or too many resources) budgeted to accomplish the marketing objectives?

B. How do you rate your effectiveness?

1. On what basis does the organization measure the effectiveness of its programs?

2. What are the major weaknesses in each program area? What are the major complaints? What goes wrong most often?

3. Does it seem that the agency is trying to do too much, or not enough?

4. Do any programs seem to have excessive costs? Are these costs valid? Can cost-reducing steps be taken?

5. Has there been a recent evaluation of the agency's existing distribution pattern of both facilities and services?

II. <u>EXTERNAL AUDIT</u>

   A. Other providers

   1. Which organizations are competing with you directly by offering a similar service?

   2. Which other organizations are competing with you indirectly by securing prime prospect's time, money, energy, and commitment?

   3. What new competitive trends seem likely to emerge?

   4. Is it appropriate for us to compete? Could you more usefully withdraw from some areas where there are alternative suppliers and use our resources to better effect to service new unserved client groups?

   5. How effective is the competition? What benefits do your competitors offer that you can not?

   B. Marketplace trends

   1. What major technological changes are occurring which affect the agency?

   2. What financing laws are now being proposed at federal, state, and local levels which could affect marketing strategy and tactics?

   3. What political changes at each government level are taking place?

C. Physical, social, and cultural factors

   1. What major social and lifestyle developments and trends will have an impact on the agency?

   2. What impact will forecasted trends in the size, age profile, and distribution of population have on the agency?

   3. What cultural features are relevant, or potentially relevant, to your services?

   4. What are the geographical features of your service area? What opportunities are created? What limitations are imposed?

   5. How good is public transportation access to facilities? Can it be improved?

III. USER/POTENTIAL USER ANALYSIS

   A. Are needs assessments undertaken? How often? When was the most recent one completed?

   B. Which are high-opportunity and low-opportunity segments?

   C. What are the evolving needs and satisfactions being sought by constituent publics?

   1. What does each segment seek from the agency?

   2. What are the major objections given by consumers as to why they do not use the agency's services?

   3. How do users find out about and decide to try and/or use the organization's services? When and where?

   4. What is the agency's image with respect to the specific market segments it seeks to serve?

   5. What are the pressures among various publics to increase or to decrease the range and/or quality of services?

6. How much of program use is repeat versus new business? What percent of the public can be classified as nonusers, light users, and heavy users?

D. What publics other than direct client groups (financial, media, government, citizen, local, general, and internal), represent particular opportunities or problems for the agency?

APPENDIX 2

MARKET SEGMENTATION

Segmentation variables
with typical breakdown

Geographic

    Zone:
      North; East; West; Central; South

    Neighboorhood:
      By name

    Density:
      Urban; suburban; rural

Demographic

    Age:
      Under 6; 6-11; 12-17; 18-34; 35-49; 50-64; 65+

    Sex:
      Male; female

    Family size:
      1-2; 3-4; 5+

    Family life cycle:
      Young, single, young, married, no children;
      young married, youngest child under 6; young,
      married, youngest child 6 or over; older,
      married, with children; older married, no
      children under 18; older single; other

    Houshold Income:
      Under $8,000; $8,000-$9,999; $10,000-$14,999;
      $15,000-$19,999; $20,000-$29,999;
      $30,000-$39,999; $40,000 +

    Occupation:
      Professional and technical; managers, officials,
      and proprietors; clerical; sales; craftsmen;

foreman; operatives; farmers; retired; students; housewives; unemployed

Education:
Grade school or less; some high school; graduated high school; some college; graduated college; postgraduate

Religion:
Catholic; Protestant; Jewish; other

Race:
Hispanic; Native American; White; Black; Asian

Nationality:
American; British; French; German; Eastern European; Scandinavian; Italian; Spanish; Latin American; Middle Eastern; Japanese

Social Class:
Lower; lower-middle; middle-middle; upper-middle; upper

Psychographic*

Life style:
Upscale; blue collar; health-oriented; etc.

Personality:
Compulsive; gregarious; conservative; ambitious; etc.

Benefits sought:
Economy; convenience; dependability; prestige; etc.

User status:
Nonuser; potential user; first-time user; regular user; ex-user

Usage rate:
Light user; medium user; heavy user

*Note: Psychographic indicators require careful professional interpretation.

Loyalty status:
  None; medium; strong; absolute

Readiness stage:
  Unware; aware; informed; interested; desirous;
  intending to buy

Selected Bibliography

GENERAL

Howard, Dennis and John Crompton, <u>Financing, Managing, and Marketing Recreation and Park Resources</u>, Wm. C. Brown Co. Publishers, Dubuque, Iowa, 1980.

Kotler, Philip, <u>Marketing Management</u>, Northwestern University, Prentice-Hall Inc., Englewood Cliffs, New Jersey, 1980.

Kotler, Philip, <u>Marketing for Nonprofit Organizations</u>, Prentice-Hall Inc., Englewood Cliffs, New Jersey, 1975.

Stanton, William J., <u>Fundamentals of Marketing</u>, McGraw-Hill Book Co., New York, 1981.

ANALYSIS

Coleman, Richard P., "The Significance of Social Stratification in Selling," in <u>Marketing: A Maturing Discipline</u>, pp. 171-84, ed. Martin L. Bell, American Marketing Association, Chicago, 1961.

Frank, Ronald E., William F. Massey, and Yoram Wind, <u>Market Segmentation</u>, Prentice-Hall, Inc., Englewood Cliffs, New Jersey, 1972.

Hanan, Mack, <u>Life-Styled Marketing</u>, American Management Association, Inc., New York, 1972.

Hatry, Harry, Louis H. Blair, Donald M. Fisk, John H. Greiner, John R. Hall, Jr., and Phillip S. Schaemen, <u>How Effective Are Your Community Services</u>? The Urban Institute, Washington, D.C., 1977.

League of Women Voters of Massachusetts, <u>Survey Savvy: A Guide For Understanding Surveys</u>, League of Women Voters, Boston, Massachusetts, 1979.

Wells, William D., "Psychographics: A Critical Review," *Journal of Marketing Research*, May 1975, pp. 196-213.

Wilkie, William L. and David M. Gardner, "The Role of Market Research in Public Policy Decision Making," in *Journal of Marketing*, 38, pp. 38-47, 1974.

STRATEGY DEVELOPMENT

Bates, Don, "How Public Relations Can Help Your Fundraising Efforts Pay Off," *Grantsmanship Center News*, Vol. 5, No. 4 (Issue 30), July - August 1979, pp. 36-41.

Bureau of Outdoor Recreation, *Evaluation of Public Willingness to Pay User Charges for Use of Outdoor Recreation Areas and Facilities*, U.S. Superintendent of Documents, Washington, D.C., 1976.

Couble, Michelle, *Effective Promotion: A Guide to Low Cost Use of Media for Community Organizations*, Do It Now Foundation, Phoenix, Arizona, 1977.

Cutlip, Scott M., and Allen H. Center, *Effective Public Relations*, Prentice-Hall, Englewood Cliffs, New Jersey.

Gordon, Robbie, *We Interrupt This Program...A Citizen's Guide to Using the Media for Social Change*, Citizen Involvement Training Project, University of Massachusetts, Amherst, Massachusetts, 1979.

Grantsmanship Center, "Guide to Public Relations for Non-Profit Organizations and Public Agencies," *Grantsmanship Center News Reprint*, Grantsmanship Center, Los Angeles, California, 1977.

Heritage Conservation and Recreation Service, *Fees and Charges Handbook*, Washington, D.C., 1979. (Available from National Park Service, Division of Park and Recreation Technical Services, Interior Building, 18th & 19th Streets at Virginia, N.W., Washington, D.C. 20240).

Kotler, Philip and William Mindak, "Marketing and Public Relations," *Journal of Marketing*, pp. 13-20, October 1978.

Levinson, Nan S., *The Logo Handbook*, Art Extension Service, Division of Continuing Education, University of Massachusetts, Amherst, Massachusetts, 1979.

National Trust for Historic Preservation, *Public Relations for Local Preservation Organizations: Press Relations, Public Education and Special Events*, National Trust for Historic Preservation, Washington, D.C., 1980.

Pawlak, Vie, *How to Publish Community Information on an Impossibly Tight Budget*, Do It Now Foundation, Phoenix, Arizona, 1976.

Public Management Institute, *Successful Public Relations Techniques*, Public Management Institute, San Francisco, California, 1980.

Public Media Center, *Strategies for Access to Public Service Advertising*, Public Media Center, San Francisco, California, 1976.

IMPLEMENTATION

Kotler, Philip, "Strategies for Introducing Marketing Into Non-Profit Organizations," *Journal of Marketing*, Vol. 43, pp. 37-94, 1979.

EVALUATION

Bloom, Paul N., "Evaluating Social Marketing Programs: Problems and Prospects," *1980 Educators Conference Proceedings*, American Marketing Association, Chicago, 1980.

II. Needs Assessment
Taking the Pulse of the Public Recreation Client

TO SERVE ALL CITIZENS,
A NEEDS ASSESSMENT MUST "TAKE
THE PULSE" OF THE ENTIRE COMMUNITY.

Introduction

WHY DO A NEEDS ASSESSMENT?

The function of any park and recreation agency is to provide the public with what they want and need. To determine exactly what these wants and needs are, an agency must undertake some form of needs assessment. That is, the agency must gather information directly from the public and subject that information to analysis. The result of this process is a consensus which can direct the agency toward fulfilling expressed needs and, in effect, guide efficient, effective, and equitable service delivery.

The consumer serves as the focus in a marketing approach. Since an agency's constituency consists of _all_ citizens, a needs assessment must "take the pulse" of the entire community, being responsive and accountable to more than just the vocal and visible interest groups of current users.

All of the marketing tasks--setting objectives, identifying target markets, developing products, and pricing, promoting, and distributing those products--assume that a needs assessment has been undertaken. For example:

* What do its constituencies believe the agency should be doing? (Setting Objectives)

* What needs and wants do citizens have? What are the characteristics of those who have a particular need? How many are affected? What makes individuals decide to use or not use existing services? (Identifying Target Markets)

* How do potential target markets react to various service alternatives that could meet these needs? (Product Development)

* What price should be charged? (Pricing)

* How can its availability be best communicated? (Promotion)

* At what time and locations should it be offered? (Distribution)

Building support constituencies is important to any public agency today, and needs assessments are key tools in achieving this. Needs assessments can provide the support data necessary for justifying requests to a political body. Not only are the findings valuable, but also the very act of doing a needs assessment is likely to demonstrate to the community and its decisionmakers that, vis-a-vis other departments, the agency did its homework. Citizens who feel they have some impact on the services being offered to them will generally react more favorably to the agency and its programs.

Consider this statement by a senior park planning official in Austin, Texas:

> In Austin we interviewed 1% of the citizens in our Needs Assessment household interviews in the summer of 1980. This doesn't sound like a very large sample, yet it seems everybody in the city knows somebody who has been interviewed. The very positive public relations effort, press support, and public response, which resulted simply from having done the needs assessment, was a bonus benefit we did not anticipate from this effort.

GENERAL APPROACHES TO NEEDS ASSESSMENT

There are four general approaches which may be used in an assessment of community needs. Three of these, citizen advisory committees, public meeting and workshops, and unstructured inputs and structured exploratory interviews are non-survey methods. Surveying is the four approach.

No one method is capable of independently producing an effective needs assessment. As will be evident from the following discussion, each method has a specific role and each makes a vital contribution.

<u>Citizen advisory committees</u>. Citizen advisory committees are generally viewed as formal (appointed or elected) bodies which link the views and opinions of different segments of the community with agency decisionmakers. They may be invaluable in providing a connection with an agency's clientele

and in assisting and supporting program planning and development. They may also be instrumental in conducting surveys and appraisals which serve as needs assessments, since they act as a liaison for screening community suggestions and criticisms.

In principle, advisory committees should reflect the different interests found among an agency's various publics and communicate the viewpoint of these interests to agency officials. They have been criticized, however, for over-representing a more affluent, influential sector of the public usually possessing more-flexible schedules, more-successful career achievement patterns, and stronger leadership voices in the affairs of the community. It would be a mistake for an agency to assume that any attempt by an advisory committee to prioritize needs incorporates the wishes of the entire community.

Still, the involvement of a citizen advisory committee can substantially enhance the quality and responsiveness of an agency's services. They may certainly be instrumental in contributing useful suggestions which help ensure that all dimensions of an issue are addressed.

In cases where the financial resources and/or the need to conduct a comprehensive needs assessment don't exist, the use of a citizen advisory committee may prove very beneficial. For conducting single-issue inquiries and small-scale surveys, ad-hoc committees may effectively provide the information desired at very little cost to the agency.

In Geneva, Illinois, a citizen advisory committee created an ad-hoc "Citizen Survey Team" which conducted an extensive telephone survey regarding parks and recreation in that community. They designed the survey and questionnaire forms, collected the data, and coordinated the analysis. Local colleges cooperated by inspecting the survey forms and methods and tabulated the results. All of this was accomplished at little cost and great benefit to the park and recreation agency.

Public meeting/workshops. A public meeting is the most common method used to solicit input from citizens on needs and preferences. It has two main advantages. First, it facilitates a two-way dialogue which enables needs to be explored at length, so that in-depth insights which help clarify and define issues more clearly may emerge. Second, personal contact transmits emotion more effectively than mail or other impersonal means of input, and it is sometimes helpful for managers to sense this emotional intensity.

Workshops are a variation of the public meeting. Participants are arranged into small discussion groups, facilitating social interaction. They focus upon identifying needs and developing program alternatives for meeting them. Workshops tend to generate more enthusiasm among participants than public meetings because participants can do more than just sit and listen.

As with citizens advisory committees, opinions expressed at public meetings or workshops are not likely to be representative of the public as a whole. Participants' input is prone to reflect the feelings of only the more active, vocal, and involved segments of the population.

Unstructured inputs and structured exploratory interviews. Unstructured inputs come from two main sources. First, unsolicited suggestions may be volunteered by citizens, usually in face-to-face meetings with employees or in telephone conversations. Second, the public may be invited to provide written input to a particular issue, after information has been disseminated through the mass media.

Exploratory interviews with selected citizens represent a more structured approach to soliciting input on needs and preferences. Those selected for interview should represent as many different relevant interest segments of the population as possible. The interview questions should be open-ended, since these interviews are "fishing expeditions" in which the intent is to catch as many different need dimensions as possible. To reduce costs, the telephone can be used as an alternative to personal interviews.

There is no simple rule for determining the number of respondents who should be interviewed. However, at a certain point, additional interviews fail to provide new insights and answers fall into a familiar pattern. Frequently, this point is reached after 15 to 20 interviews.

An alternative to individual exploratory interviews is the focus group discussion. A divergent group of citizens is brought together and a moderator generates discussion by a few carefully selected "focusing questions." The participants' statements are carefully and accurately recorded and subsequently analyzed to identify all components of the issue. Such discussion should be as expansive as possible, so that the full range of participants' opinions are revealed.

Surveys. In its final form, the survey represents a synthesis of information which emerges from the other non-survey methods. It takes all of the resulting viewpoints and issues and seeks to determine how they are distributed in the total population.

This handbook features the survey methods of needs assessment because it has been found to be the most accurate way of identifying community needs, wants, and preferences. If the survey is done correctly, the information it yields represents the views of all citizens.

<u>The approaches in concert</u>. If the four methods of needs assessment were arranged in order of amount of citizen involvement, it would form a pyramid such as in the following figure.

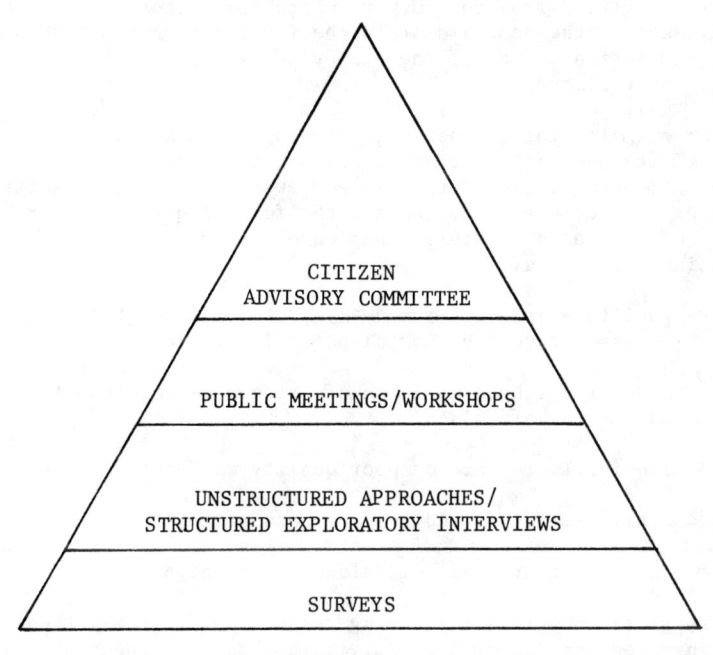

```
         /\
        /  \
       /    \
      / CITIZEN \
     /ADVISORY COMMITTEE\
    /--------------------\
   /                      \
  /  PUBLIC MEETINGS/WORKSHOPS \
 /------------------------------\
/  UNSTRUCTURED APPROACHES/      \
/ STRUCTURED EXPLORATORY INTERVIEWS \
/------------------------------------\
/            SURVEYS                   \
/_____\
```

CITIZEN INVOLVEMENT PYRAMID

More people are likely to be involved in the decisionmaking process through the use of surveys than by the use of any of the other three approaches. As was seen in the discussion of individual methods, participants of citizen advisory committees, or at public meetings or workshops, are unusually

67

motivated citizen representatives, and their inputs cannot be expected to accurately represent the priority or weighting of specific needs which would be given if inputs were obtained from all citizens in the community.

The value of the non-survey methods cannot be underestimated; their use is essential before any survey can be undertaken. Together, their role is to solicit citizen input which will expand the agency's understanding of the problem. Agency staff cannot be expected to have knowledge of all aspects of an issue, and citizens often have different perspectives of needs than agency personnel. Without direct citizen input, it is likely that some initial dimensions of the needs assessment will be omitted from the survey, which means they will not be addressed in the analysis or in the final recommendations and program actions. Hence, the survey's results will be inherently biased.

As an example, let us assume that an agency wants to increase use of its underutilized services, but does not undertake public meetings, exploratory interviews, or consult an advisory board. Agency staff may suspect the following reasons for lack of use based on their experience and the reported findings of others:

* Facilities are too far away, or too difficult to access for some groups of potential users.

* Some groups have no means of transportation to get to service offerings.

* The facilities are of poor quality and unattractive.

* Staff are not friendly or responsive to clients.

* Costs of travel or admission are too high.

Appropriate questions reflecting these suspicions may then be inserted into a survey. Survey results will identify which constitute the most substantial barriers. The department then develops an action plan aimed at reducing the impacts of the most substantial barriers, thereby increasing usership.

But the department's action plan may miss the mark, since the agency failed to solicit input from citizens. If it had sought their input, citizens may have suggested other major reasons for limited or non-use, such as lack of interest in existing offerings, negative feelings about others who participate in programs, and concern for personal safety at facilities.

Since these limiting factors were not explored in the survey, they could not be included in the action plan, based on the survey's findings, which seeks to reduce the impact of constraints. Hence, these problems, which may be of greater importance than those included in the survey, will remain unaddressed.

Preparing to Do a Needs Assessment Survey

When an issue has been fully defined with citizen input and the agency believes it is aware of all needs and viewpoints, then it is in a position to undertake a needs assessment survey. A survey is the single best approach to assessing citizens' needs and preferences if it is done right, but many surveys are of no value. These fall into one of two categories:

1. They are <u>useless</u>, in that they don't provide management with information that can be used to improve service delivery.

2. They misinform and mislead. Doing a survey poorly may be worse than doing no survey at all. It's not just a waste of time and energy--it may send your agency shooting off in the wrong direction.

Survey results may be biased, and thus misinform, because low response rates are obtained, or because of the way in which questions are written, the way they are asked, and the method by which respondents are selected to receive the survey.

If all of the people in a population are interviewed, then the survey is called a census. Usually, neither the time nor the resources are available to make a census, so only a sample of the population is interviewed and their answers are used to represent the whole population. A sample survey is like taking a spoonful of soup from a bowl. If the soup has been thoroughly stirred, then this spoonful will give an accurate representation of the soup's taste without having to drink the whole bowl. Similarly, for a sample survey of residents to be representative, members of the population to be included in the sample must be selected according to various statistical techniques in such a way that they represent the entire population.

WHY DON'T AGENCIES MAKE MORE USE OF NEEDS ASSESSMENT SURVEYS?

The value of needs assessment surveys seems obvious. Nevertheless, many agencies never untake them. Surveys are either ignored or else carried out in a perfunctory way. Why?

A SURVEY SAMPLE IS LIKE TASTING SOUP. IF THE SOUP HAS BEEN THOROUGHLY STIRRED, ONE SPOONFUL WILL GIVE AN ACCURATE IDEA OF THE SOUP'S TASTE

LACK OF SELF-CONFIDENCE is one reason. To many, research appears frightening and complex. Don't be intimidated! The complexity usually revolves around the use of advanced statistical techniques which are not necessary for your purposes.

LACK OF TIME OR MONEY is many times cited as a prohibiting factor. A needs assessment does take time and money, but not as much of either as most people imagine. In view of the potential benefits to effective decisionmaking, the investment in time and money is well spent.

Another reason given is SERVICE OVERLOAD. A survey generally raises the expectations of citizens, who expect their particular service requests to be optimally met. Managers often say, "We're serving more people than we can handle right now, we sure don't need to take on any new prospects." In fact, the elimination and reduction of services is as much a concern in needs assessments as the expansion and development of new services. Assessments may provide the evidence necessary to demonstrate why resources should be reallocated.

Some agencies point to the need to maintain SERVICE STANDARDS. While standards offer a good yardstick for measuring overall service levels, it is really people that are the focus and purpose of a parks and recreation system, not facilities, and their needs are not standardized. Needs assessments indicate how the public's diverse needs and preferences can be met.

DISAPPOINTING EXPERIENCES sometimes cause a hesitancy to pursue another needs assessment. However, if previous assessments have been disappointing, it may be that the problem lies in the way the survey was conducted, not with the approach. Review past efforts and make the necessary adjustments.

There are trade-offis, because doing a needs assessment means taking resources away from some other effort. To be successful, a needs assessment survey requires an extensive commitment from administrators. The information gained can, however, ultimately save an agency time and money, and lead to the best possible program decisions.

WHAT DO YOU WANT TO LEARN FROM THE NEEDS ASSESSMENT SURVEY?

Determining the specific purpose of the survey is the important first step in the entire process. Do not begin a needs assessment survey until you can state in writing why it is being done. Without this very specific clarity of purpose at the outset, your survey is likely to join the many surveys which are shelved when completed because the information was not in a form the agency could use. Be sure that you're not doing the survey because "it would be nice to know something about our customers" or "it seems like a good idea to get the public involved."

Give considerable time and thought to the purpose and specific use which will be made of the information the survey will yield. Setting specific, rather than general, objectives for the survey is an often difficult but crucial task; it dictates the questions which are to be included and the usefulness of the data. If the stated goals are too broad and general, the survey's results are likely to be difficult to interpret and implement because they don't relate to specific issues.

Here are some of the objectives used by the Austin, Texas, Parks and Recreation Department (PARD) to guide its needs assessment surveys:

Overall Objectives

1. To provide the data necessary to facilitate development of the Department's new master plan.

2. To solicit information which will assist in making future management and/or marketing decisions.

Specific Objectives

1. To identify the priorities of citizens in each geographic zone and in different sociodemographic groups for:

    a) new or renovated facilities, amenities, and services in their planning district

    b) the allocation of PARD tax funds to the various types of services the department offers.

2. To solicit citizen guidance as to the future direction of the Department as a provider, facilitator, or outreach agency.

3. To increase understanding of why many citizens of Austin do not take advantage of the services/ facilities offered by the Department.

4. To identify the level of prices acceptable to users of specific types of recreation facilities and services.

5. To identify the level of tax support acceptable to non-users of specific types of recreation facilities and services.

6. To identify the extent of constituency use and support for each of the types of services offered by the Department.

No attempt was made to meet all of the specific objectives in one survey. If this were done, the limited information gained in each area could only be general and superficial. Rather, each of these objectives served to guide and direct a separate needs assessment survey, so sufficient understanding could be gained in each area to enable management decisions to be made with confidence.

WHICH SURVEY METHOD SHOULD BE USED TO COLLECT THE INFORMATION?

Four major alternative survey methods may be used to gather information for needs assessments: 1) mail questionnaire, 2) personally delivered self-administered questionnaire, 3) telephone interviews, and 4) personal interviews.

No one method can be considered "best" in all situations. The objectives of the study, the nature of the information to be gathered, and the resources available will help decide which method is most useful. The following paragraphs briefly identify the major advantages and disadvantages associated with each method.

<u>Mail questionnaire</u>. Using this method, the questionnaire is mailed to the sample, accompanied by a cover letter briefly explaining the survey's purpose, the agencies involved, and the importance of the contact's response. A self-addressed stamped envelope is enclosed. Since mail questionnaires often have low response rates, using a business-reply mailing permit is likely to be least expensive since the charges are imposed only for the questionnaires returned.

Advantages:

* Least expensive of all methods to reach selected respondents.

* Can contact large numbers of households in an extended geographical area.

* Requires least manpower and skill to administer, and eliminates the need for training interviewers.

* Enables a respondent to reflect on questions before responding.

* Most likely to be successful in obtaining input from all family members, if such information is sought.

Disadvantages:

* Low rate of return. Mail questionnaires sent to a general public often have response rates of 30%-35%. This percentage is likely to be even lower if the survey is simply included with a utility bill or similar notice, since the questionnaire may then receive only secondary attention.

* The problem with low response rates is that those who complete the survey may have very different reactions than those who did not respond. Typically, the low-income, low-education, older, and non-user segments of the population are less likely to respond to a survey. Hence, the results may be biased and the information of doubtful value. There are three ways in which this problem can be attacked:

    1. Oversample the groups least likely to respond.

    2. Send follow-up letters with another questionnaire to those who don't respond.

    3. Sample those who don't respond to see if their opinions differ from those who do respond.

* Delay in receiving completed questionnaires. If two follow-ups are used, the time between the first mailing and an effective end of the returns may be two or three months.

<u>Personally delivered self-administered questionnaire</u>. In this case, a questionnaire is personally handed to respondents at their home or on-site. Respondents are informed of the study's purpose and a commitment is sought from them to complete

* The major cost is paying the telephone interviewers. If existing staff can be temporarily assigned to this task, then the additional cost to the agency of doing the survey is minimal.

Disadvantages:

* Excludes those who do not have phones. In most areas, phones are owned by over 95% of households. The households without phones are likely to be low-income, so some over-sampling of low-income households may be required to ensure they are adequately represented.

* If the sample is selected randomly from the phone book, those with unlisted numbers will be excluded. The number of unlisted numbers may be significant in some urban areas. However, this problem may be overcome by selecting respondents by randomly dialing within a telephone exchange district, rather than using the phone book.

* Interview length is limited. For phone interviews, 10-15 minutes should be considered the maximum length. This time limit is a good rule of thumb for any kind of survey.

* Young people and females are more likely to answer household phones than other members of the family; therefore, the sample may not be representative.

<u>Personal interviews</u>. A personal interview is conducted on a face-to-face basis by an interviewer who verbally administers the questionnaire. Such interviewers need to be trained in the specifics of the questionnaire and in interview procedures. Details of appropriate training are described in Appendix 1.

Advantages:

* Response rates are likely to be high, frequently 85%-90%. Respondents are less likely to turn down an interviewer on their doorstep than they are to throw away a mail questionnaire or hang up a telephone.

* More-complex information can be gathered because it can be explained to respondents and, if necessary, the survey's lanaguage can be adapted to meet the educational level of respondents. Visual material can also be used in the interview.

the questionnaire within a given time period. This advanced commitment, and the personal contact, usually leads to a substantially higher proportion of questionnaires being returned than would be achieved by mailing the questionnaire. A less-effective approach than personal delivery (which nevertheless is an improvement on simply mailing the questionnaire) is to telephone intended recipients, seeking a commitment that the questionnaire will be filled out before mailing it to them. The questionnaire can also be picked up personally by a staff member, mailed back in a return envelope which is provided, or handed in at a deposit box situated within the facility, usually at an exit point.

The pros and cons of this approach are similar to those of mail questionnaires, with the following exceptions:

Advantage:

* Higher return rates. Typically response rates of 50%-75% are achieved, depending upon which return method is used.

Disadvantages:

* Increased costs are incurred by the need to travel and to use more employee time to delivery (and, in some cases, to pick up) the questionnaires.

* In on-site surveys, it is difficult to distribute the questionnaires so that a representative sample of users is selected.

Telephone interviews. Use of the telephone to conduct needs assessment surveys has increased in recent years primarily because phone interviews are more convenient and lower in cost than personal interviews.

Advantages:

* The logistics and supervision are easier to manage than other approaches.

* Response rates are higher than mail questionnaires. These rates range from 35%-50% of those contacted.

* Information is collected faster than by any of the other methods.

Disadvantages:

* The major disadvantage is cost, which is much higher than for the other methods.

* If household interviews are conducted during the normal 8:00 to 5:00 work period, a biased sample will result. Housewives will make up the majority of the sample and working males and females will be almost totally excluded.

HOW MUCH WILL IT COST?

Clearly, it is difficult to generalize about costs. However, before a survey is undertaken, some determination must be made of at least the broad parameters of cost and staff time which may be committed to the project, since this will impact many subsequent decisions in implementing the survey. The main expenditures in a needs assessment survey tend to be for:

* Overall supervision and planning by the project director (and possible fees to consultants)

* Training and Supervision of the interviewers

* Salaries of the interviewers

* Verification and coding of the questionnaire

* Mechanical and electronic data processing

* Secretarial and clerical services

* Supplies

The cost of a needs assessment survey may range from a few hundred to tens of thousands of dollars. The actual cost in any given situation depends upon the type of survey, the size of the sample, and the length of the questionnaire.

The most expensive type of survey involves contracting with an experienced professional market research company. Typically, the company would be required to design the questionnaire, select the sample, collect the data, and provide frequency distributions and cross-tabulations of the results. Companies do not usually undertake further analysis or provide any discussion of the implications of the data. The following average prices were compiled from quotes provided by professional market research firms early in 1981. They assume a sample size of 300 (a typical number) and a questionnaire which takes 10 minutes to complete:

	Total Cost	Per Person Contact Cost
Mail Questionnaire	$2,700	$ 9
Telephone Interviews	$5,500	$18.33
Personal Interviews	$22,000	$73.33

It should be noted that these are contact costs, not response costs. Mail questionnaires appear to be the least expensive, but if only 50% of those surveyed return their questionnaires, then the per-response cost of the mail questionnaire rises from $9 to $18. If the response rate falls to 33% (which is not unusual), then the pre-response cost increases to $27. In such situations, telephone interviews may be less expensive.

The telephone and personal interviews assume a 90% incidence; that is, that 90% of people selected in the sample will be home and available when the telephone call or personal visit is made. If the incidence rate is lower, and more than 10% of the sample require follow-up calls or visits to secure their response, the price would increase. The personal interview cost assumes that the sample is random. If it were clustered, then this would reduce costs. (This is discussed later in the section on sampling).

Using a professional market research firm to do a needs assessment survey is likely to produce the best results, for such companies have the expertise to ensure that the information which is collected is valid and representative. Such firms can be expensive, and some agencies may have difficulty in persuading their Board to make an investment of this magnitude. The alternatives include:

* Using existing staff to do the needs assessment in-house. This assumes the expertise is available.

* Hiring additional temporary staff to do the survey.

* Soliciting and obtaining a donation of the needed expertise from a major corporation. This is exactly the kind of assistance many corporations are willing to provide to public agencies.

* Contracting with a local university to assist with the project. The Marketing, Political Science, Sociology, and Recreation and Park Departments of universities frequently are looking for "live" research projects in which to involve their graduate students. The agency should check that the professor is knowledgeable and experienced in doing needs assessment surveys. Given that condition, since it is a legitimate and exciting learning experience for students, the cost of their labor will be low.

The Austin Park and Recreation Department used a combination of three of these alternatives to undertake a major needs assessment survey. The existing staff provided overall direction to the study, managed the logistics and resources, and guided administrative and supervisory functions throughout the data-collection process. Additional temporary staff were hired to conduct personal interviews and implement public-involvement procedures.

A faculty member and five graduate students from a local university designed and pilot-tested the questionnaires, analyzed the data, and produced reports stating the findings, conclusions, and implications.

Several different types of surveys were used, including 3,600 personal household interviews; 2,600 personally delivered, mail-back questionnaires; 990 on-site personal interviews; and 700 questionnaires completed by grade school students in their classrooms.

The approximate costs of this total project conducted in the summer of 1980 were:

Existing staff in-house time	$50,000
Temporary staff hired for the needs assessment (interviewers, resident aides, coders, etc.)	41,000
Local university faculty member and graduate student in-kind time	15,000
Supplies (computer time, printing, postage, etc.)	10,000
Total	$116,000

Does this cost sound exorbitant? Think about it in proportion to your own agency. Including all the in-kind labor time devoted to the project, it represents 1.25% of the Austin Park and Recreation Department's annual operating budget, and amounts to 33 cents per resident. If annual capital improvement expenditures were included, this percentage would be even lower. Few successful commercial enterprises would consider spending so little on market research. They recognize that to remain successful in today's dynamic marketplace, a substantially greater proportion of their budget must be invested in research.

HOW LONG WILL THE SURVEY TAKE?

The time period needed to do a survey depends upon the survey method used, the resources available, the level of detail required in the analysis, and the length of the questionnaire. The mail questionnaire is likely to require the longest time period, several months. Time must be allocated for:

* Designing and pre-testing the questionnaire.

* Obtaining sampling frames and selecting the sample.

* Preparing the surveys for mailing.

* Questionnaires to be returned (about two weeks for each mailing).

* Coding and analyzing the data.

* Writing the report and presenting the findings.

Telephone surveys and personal interviews generally take less time, but as was noted earlier, they may be more costly in other ways.

It is reasonable to anticipate that a period of six to nine months may be required from the initial decision to proceed with a survey to final production of the report describing the analyses, findings, and application.

MANAGEMENT OF INTERVIEWERS

If a mail survey is used, no interviews are required. However, use of telephone or personal interview involves the agency in the recruitment, remuneration, training, management, and monitoring of interviewers.

The following are helpful tips for managing interviewers:

* Hire experienced interviewers (such as prior Bureau of Census canvassers) when possible.

* Provide sufficient orientation and initial training.

* Interviewers should, if possible, be culturally representative of the survey area and respondents.

* A field pilot test (pre-test) should be conducted to pre-test the survey methodology and interviewers' proficiencies.

* Survey the easiest areas first and incrementally move on to the more difficult. This gives the interviewers valuable experience.

* Be prepared for drop-outs and provide for substitutes.

* Meet routinely with interviewers to discuss problems and provide additional training.

* Provide a reasonable, equitable pay rate to the interviewers.

SO WHICH SURVEY METHOD SHOULD I USE?

The selection of a specific survey method will depend on which factors or characteristics are salient to the purpose of the survey. As was stated at the beginning of this section, no one method is "best" in all situations. However, in most cases the personal interview is the most accurate and reliable approach.

In Austin, the Parks and Recreation Department concluded that home interviews were the only way to gather the depth and breadth of information required. The survey used photographs to seek citizen guidance in determining appropriate maintenance levels for parks, and this could only be done with personal interviews. In addition, some of the questions were complex and needed further explanation in some of the lower socioeconomic areas of the city.

Any number of combinations of survey methods may be employed. The purpose of the survey and the agency's capabilities determine what is best for that agency's particular needs.

Designing the Questionnaire

Information is collected from respondents through the use of a questionnaire. This can be geared to whichever survey method is to be used, (i.e., mail, drop-off, telephone interview, or personal interview). Detailed discussion of questionnaire design is beyond the scope of this handbook. However, the major points which must be addressed are briefly described in this chapter.

Designing an effective questionnaire can be a frustrating task. It takes effort and time, and should not be rushed. But remember, all of the resources invested in collecting, analyzing, and presenting the information will not pay off if the questionnaire is not carefully and systematically developed.

Samples of needs assessment questionnaires for recreation and park departments are included in Appendix 2. The issues and concerns are never the same in any two communities. Each agency has to tailor needs assessment surveys to the unique set of conditions existing in its community. However, it is futile to re-invent the wheel; the format, instructions, sequencing patterns and wording used successfully by others may be adapted for use in your own survey.

INTRODUCTORY COMMENTS AND THE COVER LETTER

The introductory comments should seek to establish the identity and legitimacy of the interviewer; communicate the purpose of the survey; motivate a respondent to cooperate; and explain to a respondent how he or she was selected.

Suggested approaches for the personal and telephone interview methods may be found in the questionnaire examples in Appendix 2. In the case of the mail questionnaire, these introductory functions are achieved by a cover letter which accompanies the questionnaire. Examples of cover letters are included in Appendix 3. This Appendix also includes a sample follow-up cover letter which is used in an effort to elicit responses from people selected as a part of the sample

question types is briefly discussed in the following paragraphs, and examples of each can be found in the questionnaires exhibited in Appendix 2.

OPEN-ENDED QUESTIONS permit respondents to reply in their own words rather than being limited to choosing among a set of alternatives. An example would be, "What is your favorite leisure activity?" A wide variety of responses may be elicited, and all dimensions of an issue may be identified. As a result, greater insight is gained into respondents' frames of reference, that is, what is most important to them and what their actual views are. These responses provide guidance for the formulation of fixed-alternative questions.

Unfortunately, the diversity of responses makes coding the data a difficult and time-consuming task. Furthermore, in interview situations, the interviewers have considerable discretion as to what is recorded, which may be a significant source of error.

FIXED-ALTERNATIVE (CLOSED) QUESTIONS offer a respondent predetermined response categories from which he or she must choose an answer. For each question, the respondent is instructed to check the box or boxes that apply. The advantages of this type of question are that they are simpler for both the interviewer and the respondent, and coding costs and time are greatly reduced. A disadvantage is that by offering fixed alternatives, respondents are forced to give an opinion about an issue on which they may really have no opinion. To avoid this, an "undecided" or "no opinion" category is generally desirable. It is also necessary that the response categories be exhaustive and mutually exclusive; no response should be able to fall into more than one category.

SCALED QUESTIONS may be viewed as another type of fixed-alternative question. For example, one of the sample questionnaires in Appendix 2 presents respondents with a series of recreation and park projects and asks them to check the level of priority which should be given to each of them by the city in spending the limited available funds. These response categories may have been given in the standard form of fixed alternatives.

IN WHAT ORDER SHOULD THE QUESTIONS BE ASKED?

The order in which questions are asked can affect the answers given. For example, if questions about park safety are asked

IN DESIGNING YOUR SURVEY, BE PARTICULARLY ALERT TO THE DANGER OF USING TECHNICAL JARGON.

who failed to respond to the questionnaire when it was first sent to them.

QUESTION CONTENT

Consider the following concerns regarding question content:

* Is the question necessary? Does it serve the objectives of the survey? The acid test is-- What will be done with the information from this question?

* Can it be answered accurately? Does it evoke an objective, unbiased answer, e.g., frequency of facility use within a given time period?

* Will respondents answer the questions? When possible, avoid sensitive questions, particularly those seeking personal information such as income. If they are necessary, place them at the end of the survey.

QUESTION PHRASING

It is imperative that the language used in the questionnaire be understood easily and uniformly by all respondents. Use the simplest wording possible which conveys the meaning intended. Words should always be keyed to the lowest educational level of the population to be questioned. For example, some of the intended sample may not understand, "What is your marital status?"

Be particularly alert to the danger of using technical jargon. Words which are part of the recreation and park professional's everyday vocabulary may be totally unfamiliar to the average citizen or may communicate something entirely different.

WHAT TYPE OF QUESTIONS CAN BE USED?

Three kinds of questions are used in needs assessment surveys: 1) open ended, 2) fixed alternative (sometimes called closed questions), and 3) scaled. Although open-ended questions are frequently used, questionnaires are most likely to be comprised predominantly of fixed-alternative or scaled types of questions, for reasons described below. Each of these

at the beginning, and respondents are asked later for reasons why they do not visit parks, it is likely that the results will show a greater emphasis on park safety, in relation to other reasons, than would otherwise be the case. It is advsiable to begin with questions which are likely to secure respondents' interest and cooperation. This is important because their first impression may determine their level of cooperation. The early questions should be non-threatening and serve to relax the respondent.

It is prudent not to ask sensitive questions, since this may alienate respondents and reduce their inclination to cooperate. If questions seeking information on such items as income or ethnicity are considered essential, then they should be located toward the end of the questionnaire. In this way, if a respondent is angered by such questions and refuses to answer the rest of the questionnaire, less information will be lost.

The questionnaire should finish with easy, non-threatening questions which provide an opportunity for "cooling off" and reduce the likelihood of a respondent having an unpleasant feeling when the questionnaire has been completed.

Finally, efforts should be made to ensure that questions proceed in a logical progression from one topic to the next, so that a respondent is not forced to mentally jump from one area to another.

WHAT DOES THE QUESTIONNAIRE LOOK LIKE?

The lay-out and appearance of a questionnaire are just as important as the content, phrasing, sequencing, and formating of the questions asked. If lay-out and appearance are poor, refusals and errors are likely to increase. Visual impact is particularly important for mail and drop-off questionnaires where respondents have to read and respond to them alone. However, even in interview situations, a cluttered, unprofessional-looking questionnaire is likely to cause trained interviewers to miss questions.

Efforts should be made to maximize the "white space" on a questionnaire to avoid a cluttered look. It should be kept short, since this will make it more likely that respondents will complete it. However, shortness should not be achieved by making it look cramped and cluttered, for this will increase the likelihood of refusal or errors. Furthermore, the respondent who has spent considerable time on the first page of what seemed to be a short questionnaire may be more demoralized than the respondent who quickly completed the first several pages of what initially seemed like a rather long one. In addition, saving space by placing two questions on a single line, abbreviating words, or omitting phrases may cause questions to be missed or misinterpreted.

Each section of the questionnaire should be headed by some general instructions indicating how the answers should be recorded. In addition to basic instructions, it is often helpful to begin each section of the questionnaire with a brief introduction explaining its content and purpose. These statements make the questionnaire appear more organized for the respondent, particularly if a number of different topics are covered.

There are three main methods available for reproducing the questionnaire. The choice depends on funds.

1. Ditto, mimeograph, and xerox copies are usually the least expensive to make, but they lack a professional appearance.

2. Photo-offsetting improves the quality, and the cost may actually be less if a substantial number of copies is required.

3. Type-setting gives the highest quality of reproduction, but is more expensive and takes longer to prepare.

The appearance of the questionnaire depends as much on the quality of reproduction as it does on lay-out. Forms prepared using higher-quality reproduction are likely to persuade more people to cooperate because they look neater and more professional. A poor job of producing the survey may convey to the respondent a lack of real concern for the information which is given. The use of colored paper for mail or drop-off questionnaires also has been shown to increase return. A light blue seems to be the most effective color.

BEWARE OF "MOTHERHOOD" QUESTIONS

Sometimes surveys ask, "What recreation activities would you participate in if they were available?" or, if a new service is proposed, respondents are often asked, "Will you use it?" Questions like these are called "motherhood" questions because they suggest an affirmative response without requiring the respondent to consider the trade-offs involved. It is likely that far more people will offer positive responses to this type of question than will actually use the services if they are offered, because no costs are attached to this use. The question is asked in a vacuum and assesses only general interest. When it comes to actually using the service, the opportunity cost of time, usage price, inadequate access to the service, lack of real motivation, or numerous other factors may cause the respondent not to follow through.

To avoid motherhood questions, be sure that the respondent is always placed in a trade-off situation. For example:

> If the money were available, the city should: (Circle only one statement)
>
> 1. Offer Service A
> 2. Offer Service B
> 3. Undecided

PRE-TEST AND REVISION OF THE QUESTIONNAIRE

After carefully crafting the questionnaire through three or four drafts to the point where the designers are satisfied with it, advice should be sought from others to further improve upon it. This advice should be solicited from four sources.

First, give the questionnaire to four or five other people from within the agency who have not been involved in its development and ask for their critical comments.

Second, ask selected citizens who are likely to be particularly knowledgeable or interested in the issues the survey addresses to critique the questionnaire. They should be asked to critique content rather than format.

Third, seek the advice of experts in questionnaire development. They may be found not only in universities and colleges, but also in the marketing departments of major local businesses. They should be asked to critique format rather than content.

Finally, the real test of a questionnaire is how it performs under the actual conditions of collecting the information. For this assessment, a pre-test of the questionnaire is essential. This involves using the questionnaire to survey a small segment of the sample population. They should be selected by drawing a sub-sample of the sample population which is to be used in the full survey.

A pre-test will always result in improvement in both the questionnaire and the techniques of administration. It is likely to reveal awkward statements or instructions; questions which are biased; the length of time it takes to complete the survey; and the level of response rate which may be expected. In addition, it gives experience to those who will distribute, collect, and code the final survey, so administrative improvements may emerge.

The results of a pre-test should be coded and cross-tabulated. These tables will confirm the need for each specific piece of information. Trial cross-tabulation will demonstrate that all data collected will be put to use and that all necessary information will be obtained.

VALIDITY AND RELIABILITY

The two prime requirements for a survey are that its findings be valid and reliable.

VALIDITY is concerned with the degree to which responses to questions measure what they are supposed to measure. Consider the example we used earlier in Chapter 2, in which an agency wants to know why citizens don't make more use of its services. Some of the possible reasons were omitted from the questionnaire, so erroneous conclusions were reached. Consequently, this survey was not valid. That is, the responses were not measuring what the agency thought they were measuring.

"Motherhood" questions, which because of their wording suggest a bias in a particular direction, also are likely to have low validity.

Assessing validity is a rather complex technical issue. Validity can never be "proved," but there is a burden on the agency doing a survey to establish that their questions accurately capture the characteristic of interest.

RELIABILITY is concerned with whether the questionnaire can produce consistent results if it is repeatedly administered. That is, would citizens give the same answers if they were asked the same question again, even by a different agency or interviewer? Reliability tries to assess how much of the variation in scores among individuals is due to inconsistencies in measurement.

It is laborious and usually impractical to survey the same person twice in order to estimate reliability of the questions. Fortunately, there are statistical methods available to assess reliability without doing this. If an experienced researcher is asked for advice before the questionnaire is administered, he or she can tell you how reliability can be assessed.

Selecting the Sample

Once it has been decided to undertake a survey, the next question to address is "Who should be surveyed?" This question should be considered in two parts: 1) How many people should be selected for the survey? 2) What methods should be used to select them?

HOW MANY PEOPLE SHOULD BE SELECTED FOR THE SURVEY?

Sampling decisions are technically complex, and if they are not correct, the findings of a survey are not likely to be useful. Experienced surveyors seek the advice of a professional statistician at this point to determine an appropriate sample size.

The agency seeks to survey as few people as are necessary to secure a satisfactory level of accuracy. Very large numbers are not likely to be required. The minimum size of the sample will vary according to the level of precision which the surveyor seeks and the method used to select respondents. Interestingly, it is incorrect to assume that a substantially larger sample is needed for larger cities. Provided a city is not extremely small, size will have very little impact upon the number of responses required in order to achieve a reasonable level of precision. For recreation and park agency needs assessment surveys, extremely high levels of precision (i.e., to within 3% accuracy) in the findings often are not necessary. A moderate error range (3%-10%) will frequently be acceptable. This means that a sample of only a few hundred citizens, if scientifically selected, is likely to be adequate to represent the whole city.

If there is an interest in differences between subgroups of the population, such as race, age, sex, areas of the city, etc., then a larger sample will be required. If the number of respondents in each subgroup is too small, then the error margin for the results relating to that subgroup may be unacceptably high. In the citizen survey completed in Austin, Texas, 3,600 interviews were conducted because the recreation and park agency wanted to examine differences in needs assessments in each of the ten zones in the city.

This meant that 350-400 people were the minimum number that could be interviewed in each zone in order for the results to be reasonably representative of the views and opinions of all the people in each zone.

SAMPLING METHODS

Sampling methods for selecting respondents are classified as either probability or non-probability. Each category has several subclassifications.

Probability sampling. The first task in probability sampling is to establish a sampling frame, i.e., the actual list from which the sample is to be selected. It may be a telephone book, a map of city streets or blocks, a voters' list, a city directory, or a registration list.

There are three main types of probability samples: random, stratified and cluster and systematic cluster. In a RANDOM SAMPLE, all units in the population have an equal chance of being chosen. A table of random numbers is frequently used to select respondents from a list of all potential candidates.

Metropolitan Dade County Park and Recreation Department in Florida used a random sample in two needs assessment surveys which they conducted in 1980. All telephone exchanges in the county, with the exception of those within the central business districts or those dedicated to a single function (for example, universities or government agencies), were identified, and this list served as the sampling frame. Respondents from at least five households in each telephone exchange area were interviewed. Non-residential household numbers were eliminated by the use of a screening question given to whomever answered the call.

Selection of households within each telephone exchange was random. A random digit dialing technique was used. A set of random numbers, consisting of four digits each, was used to select the last four digits of each number dialed. The household member who answered the phone was interviewed if he or she sounded as though they were at least 18 years of age.

A STRATIFIED SAMPLE is used when proportionate representation is sought from various segments of the population. This technique entails dividing the population into groups or strata based upon some characteristic. Examples of strata may be age strata (18-25, 26-35, 36-45, etc.), income strata (less than $9,000, $9,000-15,000, $16,000-23,000, etc.), or activity strata (golfers, tennis players, swimmers, park goers, etc.). Once the strata have been identified, a predetermined number of respondents are randomly selected from each stratum.

For example, in the Dade County study described above, the basic sampling procedure was slightly modified in order to ensure an adequate number of respondents from minority groups to make the analysis representative. In a previous 1979 study undertaken by the Department, for which the data were also gathered by telephone, the final sample reflected an undersampling of Blacks, and to a lesser extent Hispanics, in proportion to their presence in the total County population (presumably because more citizens in these groups did not possess a telephone). Accordingly, while at least five responses were gathered from each telephone exchange, those exchanges which previously had been found to have a higher proportion of minorities were oversampled in an attempt to offset the undersampling which had occurred in the 1979 survey.

The Park and Recreation Department of Revere, Massachusetts conducted a stratified survey concerned with public playgrounds in the city in 1980. A consultant was employed to conduct telephone surveys of people in the community over 18 years of age. This was supplemented by personal interviews with grade school students to gather specific user information about public playgrounds. The children were, in effect, a stratum targeted for a particular viewpoint.

CLUSTER SAMPLING entails sampling from a universe of groups rather than a universe of individuals. There are two types of cluster samples, area or geographic and systematic. The area cluster sample frequently selects groups of city streets, blocks, or census tracts. This technique is often used when personal interviews are conducted. By selecting clustered groups of people to be interviewed, substantial savings in travel costs and time can be realized. To interview a similar number of people who all live in different parts of the city would be much more expensive.

The City of Austin used this method in the first part of its procedure for selecting the sample for a city-wide needs assessment, which was conducted by personal interview. The clusters were city blocks. It was estimated that the budget limits would permit 400 interviews to be conducted in each of the ten planning zones into which the city was subdivided. Within each of these zones, all residential blocks were located on a census map. The map identified each city

residential block. The blocks were assigned a sequential
number from 1 through N (N being the total number of blocks
in the zone). Random numbers were generated by a computer
program to obtain 87 random numbers within the range 1
through N. The first 57 of these numbers were used to select
the blocks to be sampled. The remaining 30 numbers were used
to select blocks which served as alternates if for some
reason one or more of the first 57 blocks was unacceptable.
The most frequent cause for rejecting a block was simply a
lack of residential dwellings on it. The census did not
distinguish between developed and undeveloped subdivisions,
and sometimes an interviewer would arrive at an assigned
block to find only an open field. A designated block was
also rejected when it contained less than seven individual
dwelling units. On each randomly selected block, seven household units were sampled. The method for determining which
seven dwellings would be sampled was to count all dwelling
units on the block and divide by seven. The resulting number
indicated how many dwelling units were to be bypassed before
sampling a unit.

A SYSTEMATIC CLUSTER SAMPLE involves selecting every Nth
subject from a list of possible candidates. The selection
of houses on each block in the above example in Austin
was carried out using this procedure. This method frequently
is adopted to select respondents from voters' lists, telephone
directories, registration lists, or tax rolls.

Non-probability sampling. Probability sampling techniques
ensure greater representativeness and are therefore usually
preferred. There may be occasions, however, when cost
limitations prohibit the use of probability sampling, or when
representativeness is not critically important. On these
occasions, a method of non-probability sampling may be
considered.

The three most commonly used non-probability methods are
convenience, judgment (sometimes called purposive), and quota
sampling. As the name implies, a CONVENIENCE SAMPLE is
selected on the basis of convenience or accessibility. For
example, a survey regarding a bond issue may be conducted
using the first 100 persons entering city hall as the
sample. In this case, some people have a very high probability
of being selected, while the probability for others is zero.
Surveys printed in newspapers are also convenience samples.
The major limitation of convenience sampling is that the
results tend to be unrepresentative. For this reason,
convenience sampling is generally considered inappropriate
except for exploratory studies and questionnaire pre-testing.

JUDGMENT SAMPLING entails selecting respondents based upon their reputation as being knowledgeable about the particular issues of concern, or because they are perceived to represent certain groups. City councilmen and community leaders, for example, might be surveyed regarding the likelihood of a particular bond issue passing. The rationale for selecting this sample would be their awareness of the voting tendencies of the public. Since judgment sample selection is subjective and not random, results cannot be assumed to be representative. For this reason, judgment sampling, too, is generally recommended only for exploratory research and questionnaire pre-testing.

QUOTA SAMPLING is perhaps the most commonly used non-probability sampling technique. It is used when there is reason to believe that some segments of the population (for example, minorities, senior citizens, or low-income groups) will be under-represented if other sampling techniques are used. It entails selecting a sample in such a way that the characteristics of interest in the needs assessment are represented in the sample in the same proportion as they exist in the population. There are similarities between quota sampling and stratified sampling techniques. Both methods involve division of the population into segments and the selection of elements from each segment. The major difference, though, is that sample elements are selected on a probabilistic basis with stratified samples, whereas they are selected by personal judgment in quota samples.

WHAT METHOD SHOULD BE USED TO SELECT RESPONDENTS?

The major distinction between the probability and non-probability categories is that in a probability sample each citizen in the population has a known chance or probability of being selected for the sample. Given this condition, probability sampling is a much more effective method for selecting study respondents, because it 1) eliminates bias which could influence the selection of sample respondents, and 2) allows the researcher to measure the precision of sample estimates.

The key to the process of probability sampling is random selection, but random sampling is costly and there are times when the level of precision required from a survey does not justify the extra cost of this method. For surveys in which a certain amount of bias can be tolerated and the cost is limited, a non-probability sample may suffice.

Completing and Evaluating the Survey

COMPLETING THE SURVEY

Following the information-gathering steps of a survey, the data must be compiled, tabulated, and analyzed for the purposes of making recommendations and, ultimately, reporting the findings and recommendations to decisionmakers.

Tabulation. Tabulation involves the manipulation of the raw data produced in the information-gathering process of needs assessment. How the data will be compiled and tabulated must be determined far in advance of the survey. Interviewing techniques, coding methods, and questionnaire design must be consistent with the type of tabulation to be done.

Essentially, tabulation is accomplished either by automated data processing or manual means. Having agency computer capability or access to shared data-processing facilities are obviously preferred alternatives to contracting with private firms, as the latter tends to be rather expensive. Universities generally have computer and statistics classes which may be able to handle the survey tabulation at little or no cost.

Questionnaire design should facilitate the tabulation method to be employed. Closed-ended questions, for instance, are necessary for automated tabulation, since no decoding or interpretation is needed. Open-ended and scaled questions require more extensive decoding and interpretation before they can be tabulated.

Analysis and recommendations. Analysis entails all of the steps which convert the tabulated data into conclusions. Data is interpreted by the agency to determine public needs and preferences, discern trends, and suggest necessary service modifications.

The overall objectives of the needs assessment are: 1) to identify problems/issues, 2) to draw conclusions based on those findings, 3) to generate policy alternatives to deal with those issues, and 4) to advance preferred alternatives or recommendations. In the case of the City of Austin, as stated in its Parks and Recreation Master Plan, "this process established a framework for development of parks and recreation policies and standards affecting future direction of the department. The policy plan, therefore, is viewed as the first major effort in preparing the Austin Parks and Recreation Plan. With official acceptance and adoption of a policy plan, the department will then receive guidance for developing an action plan."

The product of the analysis step, then, is a list of recommended actions. The list describes actions that will be taken to ensure that the agency is providing the types and level of services which the public has indicated, through the needs assessment, that it wants. Recommendations are presented in a report of the findings.

Reporting the findings. Once the survey has been completed, tabulated, and interpreted, it should have answered the questions which it was designed to address.

A report of the findings should be prepared. Recommendations may take many forms, and are made by and to a variety of individuals and groups. Typically, a park and recreation staff will be making recommendations to its board or a governmental body with oversight authority.

The report is vital to the success of the research effort. No matter how good the needs assessment effort, if the findings are not read by the decisionmakers, or if the results are misinterpreted, then the work has been largely wasted.

Reports are often criticized as being too long and too technical. A good needs assessment report should not be criticized on either of these criteria. It is unforgivable to bore the readers of a report by making it turgid and unreadable. The writers should set forth the problem and findings from the perspective of the reader and his or her need for information. The inclination to report at length the details of technique and methodology should be resisted. The details are usually best relegated to the appendix.

The final report is written to communicate. It does not seek to be a literary production. Language should be used which is familiar to the reader and the use of technical language and professional jargon should be minimized.

The nature of the intended audience should dictate the structure and style of the report. Findings and recommendations

**THE READER WILL BE DISCOURAGED
IF THE REPORT IS TOO
FORMIDABLE IN SIZE.**

may be reported for various purposes: briefing decisionmakers, providing information for press releases, reporting to political bodies, and following up and/or reporting back to respondents.

The report should begin with what is often called an "executive summary." This includes a brief statement of the purpose of the study, methodology, findings, conclusions, and recommendations. The summary is the most important part of the report. It does not attempt to summarize everything in it, but seeks only to give the highpoints of most interest to the intended audience. Executive summaries are prepared because many people have neither the time nor the interest to read a detailed report to learn what was done and what was found.

The report should be written objectively, giving facts rather than personal judgements. Normally, reports are written in the third person, eliminating the need to use "I" or "we." The past tense is most commonly adopted because the writer is describing an activity which has already taken place.

Appearance of the report is important. If it doesn't look good, its credibility will be challenged. The appearance of the report is the reader's first impression of it and influences the state of mind with which it is read.

If the report is formidable in size it will discourage the reader. Copies of data-gathering instruments and details of data analysis should always be included in technical appendices, not in the body of the report. This provides the reader access to the information without interrupting the narrative flow of the report. Be sure to point out briefly the shortcomings and limitations of the research so the reader is not misled, particularly with regard to weaknesses in sampling or data-collection procedures.

Finally, most readers find charts and graphs more helpful than tables and statistics. Any findings that lend themselves to charts, maps, diagrams, or similar techniques should be illustrated. The cliché "one picture is worth a thousand words" is certainly applicable to needs assessment reports.

EVALUATING NEEDS ASSESSMENT STUDIES

The final step in a needs assessment, regardless of which method is used, is to evaluate the effectiveness of the survey.

Familiarity with the major steps in the research process enables the effective manager to provide input into planning needs assessment efforts and in evaluating their results. Appendix 1 is intended to provide a structured framework for these purposes.

EPILOGUE

Needs assessment is a process, not just a product. And it is an on-going process, for staying in touch with your clients is a continuous responsibility. The desires and preferences of your users are continually changing. Your services should change with the needs of your clients. This is the essence of client orientation.

The needs assessment is crucial to the effectiveness of your marketing program. Even beyond that, the process is valuable in and of itself. Through the needs assessment process, you will develop a closer relationship with your users and certainly know more about them. You will also have a better idea of how well your agency is doing its job of serving them.

Give needs assessment a try. It's one of the key first steps to client-oriented service. See what it can do for you.

Appendices

APPENDIX 1

A CHECKLIST FOR EVALUATING NEEDS ASSESSMENT SURVEYS

If the answers to all appropriate questions are yes," the chances are very good that the research being evaluated will serve its designated purpose. Any questions that must be answered "no" should lead to appropriate revisions. "Don't know" responses should be investigated further by seeking the assistance of others expert in the field of needs assessment. (This figure has been adapted from Stephen Isaac and William D. Michael, Handbook in Research and Evaluation, San Diego: Robert R. Knapp, 1971.)

	Yes	No	Don't Know	Comments

1. Was the problem and/or purpose of the study clearly and accurately stated?

2. Were specific information needs clearly and accurately stated?

3. Were the issues selected for study relevant and clearly defined?

4. Does the value of the information exceed its cost?

5. Are assumptions clearly and accurately stated?

		Yes	No	Don't Know	Comments
6.	Are limitations clearly and accurately stated?				
7.	If secondary data were used, were they:				
	(a) reasonably current?				
	(b) impartial?				
	(c) accurate?				
8.	If primary data were used:				
	(a) were acceptable secondary data unavailable?				
	(b) were data-collection procedures clear and appropriate?				
	(c) were data-collection methods used properly?				
	(d) were interviewers or observers properly selected and trained?				
	(e) were interviewers or observers adequately supervised?				

	Yes	No	Don't Know	Comments

(f) was their work validated?

9. If surveys were used:

(a) were questions simple, precise and easy to understand?

(b) were questions unbiased?

(c) could respondents reasonably be expected to provide meaningful answers to all questions?

(d) were survey instruments pretested?

10. If sampling was used:

(a) was the study population properly defined?

(b) was the sample size sufficient?

(c) was the sampling procedure appropriate?

(d) was non-response bias investigated?

11. Were appropriate data-analysis techniques selected?

		Yes	No	Don't Know	Comments
12.	Are the results of the analysis presented clearly?				
13.	Are conclusions clearly stated?				
14.	Are conclusions substantiated by the findings?				
15.	Is the report clearly written?				
16.	Is the report logically organized?				
17.	Is the report objective and unbiased?				
18.	Are details necessary to evaluate the study included in the text or in appendices?				
19.	Does the report include an executive summary?				

APPENDIX 2

SAMPLE QUESTIONNAIRES

1. Capital and Operating Priorities (telephone interview)

2. Constraints, i.e., Why Citizens Do Not Make More Use of Park and Recreation Services (telephone interview)

3. Neighborhood Capital and Operating Priorities (personal interview)

4. Delivery Service Instrument, i.e., What Types of Services and Delivery Modes Do Citizens Prefer? (personal interview)

5. Park Maintenance, i.e., How Well Satisfied Are Citizens With Existing Maintenance Efforts and What Type of Park Maintenance Do They Prefer? (personal interview)

6. Motivation, i.e., What Benefits Do Citizens Seek From Their Park and Recreation Activities? (personal interview)

NOTE: Each of these questionnaires includes a section which asks how frequently respondents participate in the services currently offered by the agency.

For the Austin, Texas, examples, the first two pages are common to all questionnaires and are introduced prior to the administration of questionnaires 3 through 6.

APPENDIX 3

SAMPLES OF COVER AND FOLLOW-UP LETTERS

SAMPLE COVER LETTER

Dear Citizen:

You have been chosen as one of a select sample of area residents.

This questionnaire is part of a study being conducted by the Department of Recreation and Parks. The goal of the study is to learn more about the recreational interests of residents in the _____ area.

If this study is to be successful, it is important that you answer each question thoughtfully and frankly. This is not a test. There are no right or wrong answers.

All individual responses are completely CONFIDENTIAL. To ensure confidentiality, please do not place your name on the questionnaire.

We need your help. Please take the next few minutes to complete the questionnaire and return it in the prepaid envelope.

Thank you for your support.

Sincerely,

SAMPLE FOLLOW-UP LETTER

Dear Visitor:

About two weeks ago we sent you a questionnaire pertaining to your visit to _____ Recreation Area. Your responses are very important to us, so we are providing you with another copy of the questionnaire in case the original copy has been lost or misplaced.

The information provided through questionnaire response will be used by the Park and Recreation Department in better serving users of _____. This is an opportunity to play a role in the management decisions of this recreation area. Returned questionnaires will be handled in strictest confidence.

If you have not already done so, please complete the questionnaire and return it in the enclosed postage-paid envelope as soon as possible. Or call us at _____ and we'll pick up the completed questionnaire.

Thank you for your interest and cooperation.

Sincerely,

Selected Bibliography

GENERAL

    Isaac, Stephen and William D. Michael, <u>Handbook in Research Evaluation</u>, Robert R. Knapp, San Diego, 1971.

    Morris, L. L. and C. T. Fitz-Gibbon, <u>Evaluator's Handbook</u>, Sage Pubs., Beverly Hills, 1978.

    Rossi, P.H. and H.E. Freeman, <u>Evaluation - A Systematic Approach</u>, 2nd edition, Sage Pubs., Beverly Hills, 1982.

    Sechrest, L., Editor, <u>Training Program Evaluators</u>, Jossey-Bass Inc., Pub., San Francisco, 1980.

SURVEYS

    Backstrom, C.H. and G.D. Hursh, <u>Survey Research</u>, Northwestern University Press, Evanston, Ill., 1963.

    Struening, E.L. and M. Guttentag, <u>Handbook of Evaluation Research</u>, Sage, Pubs., Beverly Hills, 1975.

    Survey Research Center, <u>Interviewer's Manual</u>, Revised Edition, Survey Research Center, Ann Arbor, 1976.

QUESTIONNAIRES

    Babbie, E.R., <u>Survey Research Methods</u>, Wadsworth Pub. Co., Belmont, CA, 1973.

    Lundegren, H.M. and P. Farrell, <u>Evaluation for Leisure Service Managers - A Dynamic Approach</u>, Saunders College, Philadelphia, 1984.

    Oppenheim, A.N., <u>Questionnaire Design and Attitude Measurement</u>, Basic Books, Inc., Pubs., New York, 1966.

SAMPLING

Hoinville, G. and R. Jowell, <u>Survey Research Practice</u>, Heinemann, London, 1977.

Moser, C.A. and G. Kalton, <u>Survey Methods in Social Investigations</u>, Second Edition, Heinmann, London, 1971.

Sudman, Seymour, <u>Applied Sampling</u>, Academic Press, New York, 1976.

Williams, Bill, <u>A Sampler on Sampling</u>, John Wiley & Sons, New York, 1978.

III. The Power of Promotion
Techniques of Publicity, Advertising, Personal Contact, and Special Promotions

THE TRUE DEFINITION OF PROMOTION IS TO FURTHER THE GROWTH OR ESTABLISHMENT OF SOMETHING.

Designing a Comprehensive Promotion Program

Is promotion a dirty word? To some people it smacks of manipulation and snake oil. Actually, the true definition of promotion is to further the growth or establishment of something. The key to whether promotion is a worthy or unworthy pursuit lies in the value of the product being promoted and the morality or propriety of the promotion methods used. Few would dispute that furthering the growth or establishment of park and recreation programs and facilities is a worthy goal. This handbook outlines the full range of promotion techniques that may be applicable to public or non-profit park and recreation agencies. Select those methods which are appropriate to your situation and eliminate those which are not, keeping in mind that the public insists on the unadulterated truth in promotional activities of public agencies. There can be no trace of manipulation, and if a public agency overstates its case, the public feels misled and betrayed.

The question of whether public agencies can effectively promote their programs and facilities in view of these constraints has been answered with an emphatic "Yes!" by park and recreation agencies across the country.

In the City of New Rochelle, New York, the CITY-FIT program, an innovative overall approach to well-being and fitness, relies heavily on a strong promotion program to get its message across. Some of the methods used include:

* A morning CITY-FIT program on a local radio station, giving one specific exercise per week.

* A daily cartoon in the local newspaper showing the same exercise.

* Tennis-on-the-streets demonstrations by CITY-FIT staff and recreation leaders.

* Presentations in junior high school assemblies and grade school classes by CITY-FIT staff.

* Guest appearances by staff members on local radio and cable television stations.

* Inserts on fitness and nutrition and other programs in local school newspapers, church bulletins, etc.

Another example is found in Seattle, Washington, where a special bus service running through the major parks of the city has been the focus of a strong promotional campaign. Some of the techniques utilized to create awareness include:

* Free publicity in daily and community newspapers.

* Free radio advertising.

* Wide distribution of the bus schedule through community centers, public agencies, and tourist accommodations.

* Posters in libraries, restaurants, community centers, and other public locations.

* Paid advertising in a local news magazine.

* Extensive use of free-lance writers and photographers, resulting in a feature article appearing in <u>Sunset Magazine</u>, which has a Seattle circulation of almost 150,000.

MARKETING ANALYSIS AND STRATEGY DEVELOPMENT

Promotion is just one part of an orchestrated marketing program. Before any promotion planning is done, it is essential to determine the park and recreation needs of the people in your service area and to carefully analyze the effectiveness of your programs and facilities in meeting those needs. You must also assess the strengths and weaknesses of other park and recreation providers in your area. Next you need to develop a strategy for offering services that yields the optimum facility and program mix, ideally distributed through your service area, with the proper pricing structure.

Only after these prerequisite steps have been taken should you begin designing your promotion program. If you fail to do your homework and begin promoting a substandard program or facility, you may succeed only in increasing the number of people having a less-than-satisfactory experience and in speeding up negative word-of-mouth advertising. You could be paying for this mistake for years.

The following sections will provide you with an overview of the process of designing a comprehensive promotion program. The identification of goals and objectives, the development of a promotion strategy, the preparation of a budget, and finally the implementation and evaluation of your promotion program will be discussed.

IDENTIFICATION OF PROMOTION GOALS AND OBJECTIVES

The overall goal of your promotion program should be to encourage the public to derive full benefit from the services you are providing. In other words, you should be striving to achieve full utilization of your programs and facilities by all segments of the population you are serving. To enable yourself to properly target your promotion efforts, you must carefully analyze present and projected use figures for each program and facility and for each segment of the population. You may find that you need to direct your promotion activities toward currently underutilized facilities or programs, new facilities or programs that you expect to be underutilized unless they are promoted, certain groups who rarely use your services, or more likely a combination of these.

After identifying what and/or who should be targeted for priority attention, determine why the public, or certain segments of the public, are underutilizing your services. Examine their attitudes toward your agency and the services it provides.

1. Are they unaware of some or all of your services?

2. Do they have a positive attitude toward your services, but just haven't gotten around to trying them out?

3. Do some of your facilities and programs have a bad reputation?

4. Does your agency have a less-than-dazzling image which fails to attract users or even discourages the public from trying out your services?

Refer to the information obtained through your needs assessment and fill in any information gaps by conducting additional interviews, public meetings, workshops, and/or surveys as needed.

Once you have established why the public is not taking full advantage of the services being provided, you must determine how your promotion program can most effectively encourage a change in public attitudes that will result in full utilization of your services. Promotion techniques can be used to accomplish any of the following functions:

* TO INFORM the public of the services you are providing. This is the most accepted role of promotion.

* TO REMIND users of the benefits they are deriving from the use of your programs and facilities.

* TO FAMILIARIZE the public with your agency and its services to reduce the fear of the unknown and to make them feel comfortable and secure with the thought of using your services.

* TO OVERCOME INERTIA by encouraging people to do things that they know would benefit them but haven't done because the rewards for doing them are long-term and the cost of doing them is immediate. For example, staying in good physical condition can be very beneficial, but adopting a regular exercise program is not always easy. Through the use of promotional techniques, the potential benefits can be vividly portrayed, helping the potential user to accept the "costs" more willingly.

* TO ADD PERCEIVED VALUE to your program or facility by associating it with favorable images and concepts. Although the service is the same as before the promotion occurs, it is perceived to be more valuable than before by the user. This is the most controversial function of promotion.

Some feel that it is inappropriate for park and recreation agencies to try to persuade the public to utilize their services, and that their promotional messages should be strictly informational. However, implicit in every communication identifying park and recreation opportunities is the notion that the agency considers the opportunity to be worthwhile. In attempting to design a perfectly straight-forward informational message containing no hint of persuasion, the author is caught in a dilemma. Language is not sterile. Words carry positive and negative connotations. The message's author is forced to select from a variety of different ways to describe the service being offered, some more appealing and persuasive than others.

On the other end of the spectrum are those who feel that advocacy advertising is an entirely appropriate pursuit for public park and recreation agencies. They cite public education campaigns designed to prevent forest fires, reduce litter, and encourage water and energy conservation as examples of universally accepted efforts to persuade as well as inform the public. There is no clearcut answer to what types of promotion park and recreation agencies should or should not engage in. It is up to you to set the tone of your promotional campaign so that it reflects the balance you find to be appropriate between bland, unnoticed announcements and slick, manipulatory sales pitches.

Once you have identified promotion objectives for each of your priority targets, circulate them for review, input, and hopefully staff consensus. Keep in mind that a good promotion program can be successful not only in generating goodwill in the community, but also in building staff morale.

DEVELOPMENT OF A PROMOTION STRATEGY

Promotion techniques fall into four major categories: publicity, advertising, personal contact, and special promotions, all of which are discussed in considerable detail in subsequent sections of this handbook. Each has its strengths and weaknesses and is particularly suitable for accomplishing certain promotional goals. A well-designed promotion program blends together a creative mix of complementary techniques. Carefully match each promotion objective with the technique or combination of techniques likely to yield the best results.

Sometimes an overall theme is selected to tie all of your agency promotions together and help them to build upon each other. Prominent examples include the use of a slogan, logo, shoulder patch, and mascot, and the displaying of a distinctive style of sign at all of your facilities. A less-noticeable example is the consistent use of a particular lettering style in all agency brochures and other written communications. Developing such themes establishes recognition for your agency's name and gives it an identity in the public's eyes and in the eyes of the elected officials holding the purse strings.

Prepare a promotion calendar for the budget year that sets target dates for completing key steps in your promotion program and assigns responsibility for each major task. Preparing a detailed calendar will force you to carefully plan every aspect of your promotion program. A promotion calendar will also enable you to track your progress as the year unfolds, and will help to avoid misunderstandings over what is expected of whom. Distribute the calendar to the staff and provide them with amendments during the year if significant changes are made.

While developing your promotion strategy, try to anticipate potential problems that might alter your promotion plans midstream. Develop contingency plans to handle possible funding cutbacks, pending legislation and court decisions, and other foreseeable circumstances that could impact your program.

Capitalize on the latest trends, fads, and themes in your short-term promotions. For example, if your swimming pool is underutilized at mid-day, capitalize on the current rage for physical fitness by promoting a swimming-at-lunch program as an exercise opportunity for workers during their lunch hour.

BUDGETING

Determining how much money should be spent on promotion is a difficult task, especially for a government agency or other non-profit organization. In theory, an organization should identify the level of spending that would result in a marginal gross benefit equal to the marginal promotion cost. The organization should then spend slightly less than this amount so that the last dollar spent on promotion produces slightly more than one dollar of benefit. In practice, however, it has proved quite difficult to determine the exact point where expenditures begin to become nonproductive. Not only is it difficult to assign dollar values to the benefits accrued from recreation promotion, but it is also very hard to measure the incremental effect of promotion.

Other, more practical methods of setting promotion budgets are used more frequently. Profit-making organizations sometimes budget a certain percentage of last year's sales, set a fixed sum per unit being produced, or spend the same amount on promotion as their leading competitors do. Park and recreation agencies may be able to adapt these methods to meet their particular needs. However, there is a more progressive technique, the objective and task method, that may prove more effective.

PROMOTIONAL MESSAGES SHOULD FOCUS ON THE BENEFITS TO THE USER RATHER THAN ON THE PROGRAMS THEMSELVES.

The objective and task method integrates the budgeting process into the comprehensive promotion program outlined in this handbook. In developing a strategy for accomplishing your promotion goals and objectives, preparation of a promotion calendar was recommended, with the setting of target dates and the assignment of responsible staff to key promotion tasks. The objective and task budgetary method carries this process one step further by calculating the cost of accomplishing each promotion task. The overall promotion budget figure is then determined by totaling the cost figures for all of the promotion tasks.

In times of tight government budgets, there may be insufficient funds in the park and recreation budget to allow implementation of an ideal promotion program. If your agency is basing its promotion budget on a percentage of its overall budget or on how much similar park and recreation agencies in the area are spending, then the effect of cutting the promotion budget becomes obscure. It cannot be assumed that absorbing a 20% budget cut by cutting the money allocated to each promotion objective by 20% will result in only a 20% reduction in effectiveness. It could very well result in each promotion effort becoming almost totally ineffective. The objective and task budgetary method allows decisionmakers to more clearly identify the effect of trimming the promotion budget. Costs can be assigned to accomplishing each of the promotion goals and objectives, and the decisionmakers can then evaluate which are priority objectives that must be tackled and which can be cut.

IMPLEMENTATION OF YOUR PROMOTION PROGRAM

Specific techniques for implementing your promotion strategy are discussed in detail in the handbook sections on publicity, advertising, personal contact, and special promotions. However, some general guidelines and suggestions for implementing your promotion program should be mentioned here.

In designing a promotional message, try to see it through the eyes of the prospective user. To be successful in attracting interest, the promotional messages must focus on the benefits to be derived by the user, rather than on the facilities and programs themselves. For example, in promoting an exercise class, don't merely relate the type of exercises you will be conducting. Instead, portray the feeling of well-being, the new friendships, and the increased self-esteem that participants will receive from the program.

Your agency image can be enhanced by adopting a dynamic, responsive posture in dealing with the public. Assume responsibility for communicating with the public rather than expecting them to seek you out. Establish direct, regular communication channels that the public can count on. Convey your concern for the needs of the community and your willingness to do something about them. Make sure that your actions as well as your words reflect a genuine sense of urgency, vitality, and enthusiasm in your programs.

Promoting recreation services generally requires more creativity than promoting more-tangible products. Recreation is a "product" that is produced and consumed simultaneously, not something that is viewed as a lasting personal possession once acquired. Try linking the intangible values of the recreation experience to a positive tangible image that can be readily recognized as having value. An insurance company selling the intangible service of financial protection has linked its product to a tangible image--"You're in good hands." The telephone company is promoting communication through the use of a tangible image--"Reach out and touch someone." A park and recreation agency might try a slogan such as "Play awhile--Grow a smile" as the theme for an advertising campaign featuring smiles on people of all ages, races, shapes, and sizes.

Before a prospective user can react to your message, it must attract their attention. It has been estimated that the public is bombarded with 1500 messages each day. To be successful, your promotional message has to stand out. Some examples of attention-grabbing features are humor or novelty in the message; the promise of distinctive benefits; the posing of questions; and the creative use of size, intensity of color, contrast in graphics, and isolation in print.

EVALUATION

Monitoring the success of your promotion program is essential to ensure that efficient progress toward your goals and objectives is being made. Unfortunately, there is no completely reliable technique for evaluating your promotion program.

One reason why measuring promotion effectiveness is so difficult is that uncontrollable outside factors often influence the results. For example, bad weather could have a devastating effect on attendance at a special event; an important sports event on a competing radio channel could reduce the audience for your radio advertisement; or an important news story might result in unusually high sales of a newspaper containing your advertisement.

In such cases, the strengths or weaknesses of the promotion's design can be overshadowed by outside influences.

Another reason that measuring promotion effectiveness is so difficult is that almost all promotional efforts require a time lag between implementation and effect. Not only is it impossible to assess the full impact of the promotion immediately following its implementation, but it is difficult to distinguish between the impact of the current promotion and previous promotions which are still remembered by the audience and are interacting with the present message.

A third factor complicating the measurement of the effectiveness of promotion techniques is that in a good promotion program, the promotion tools are designed to work together to achieve the target objectives. It is often difficult to determine which promotion device played the greatest role in creating the desired effect.

Many park and recreation agencies conduct their own promotion program evaluation, utilizing a "hit and miss" technique in which they try different promotion mixes until they find one that seems to achieve their goals fairly efficiently. This may prove reasonably effective if the agency is conscientious in evaluating the degree of success it has had in meeting its goals and objectives. A well-designed self-evaluation program includes (a) the establishment of measurable standards or benchmarks prior to the implementation of the promotion program and (b) the establishment of an ongoing data-collection system.

The data-collection system should be designed to provide both baseline data depicting the circumstances prior to the implementation of the promotion program and follow-up data showing the changes resulting from the agency's promotion activities. The data system should not be so narrow in scope that it measures only how successful your agency has been in meeting its planned objectives. Reaching primary promotion goals does not assure that the overall impact of the promotion will be positive. You must also assess what unintended impacts your promotion program might have had. Did you succeed in attracting a target group which had been underutilizing your facility only to discover that your promotion also resulted in a reduction in use by some other group? Did your promotion result in an increase in the number of users, but a decrease in the perceived quality of the recreation experience? Were those attracted by your promotion disappointed in their visit because they felt that they were misled by your promotion? Sometimes the importance of such side-effects can be more significant in the long-term than whether or not you met your planned objective.

The section on advertising in Part II of this handbook describes a few additional techniques for evaluating the effectiveness of your advertising program. However, if you want to undertake a more sophisticated evaluation program, you may want to seek either paid or donated professional assistance. Public relations firms sometimes utilize more intricate evaluation techniques than those commonly used by small businesses, governmental agencies, or private non-profit enterprises that conduct their own internal evaluations.

An In-Depth Look at Key Promotion Techniques

PUBLICITY

Publicity is non-sponsored media communication that brings a person, place, or cause to the attention of the public. Common types of publicity are news stories, human-interest feature stories, and other items in newspapers, radio, television, and magazines.

For many organizations, publicity, whether good or bad, is something that simply happens to them. For an organization well-versed in the inner workings of the media, publicity becomes something which is sought or avoided. Although free publicity cannot be controlled the way advertising can, it can be encouraged or discouraged utilizing the techniques discussed below.

Examples of organizations which have successful publicized their programs abound. For instance, the Seattle Parks Special bus loop that services the major parks of the city was featured in an article published in Sunset Magazine, a western-based regional magazine with a Seattle circulation of almost 150,000.

The East Bay Regional Park District in California videotapes special events, such as a park opening, and distributes the tape to networks unable to attend but wishing to report the event. In Dade County Florida, the public information officer hand-delivers press releases to the appropriate newspaper editor. The announcements appear in the newspaper, and the public information officer continues to build a solid rapport with the media.

Media contacts. The first step toward encouraging positive publicity is the identification of media contacts. Separate contact lists should be compiled for all of the various types of media that you want to have publicize your programs. Your lists may include:

  1. One small, select contact list for those who should receive every public relation item you disseminate;

2. the local daily newspapers and weekly newspapers, including toss-aways and penny savers (you may want separate lists for the city, sports, entertainment, and photo editors, and for reporters who are generally assigned to cover park and recreation, environmental, or human-interest stories);

3. local radio and television news reporters and producers;

4. local ethnic newspapers and radio and television shows;

5. local radio and television public-affairs producers;

6. national radio and television public-affairs producers;

7. wire services and nationally distributed newspapers and magazines;

8. regionally distributed newspapers;

9. columnists and commentators who might be sent small items on a rotating basis;

10. homeowner association newsletter editors;

11. local, regional, and national trade publications and corporate in-house publications;

12. friendly and related organizations that publish newsletters; and

13. funding agencies and other organizations, government bureaus and agencies, and legislators.

The following tips may be helpful in preparing your contact lists:

* Use another organization's list as a model.

* Contact the United Way or your local radio and television station public-affairs directors to see if they have an updated list of radio and television public-affairs programs and producers.

* Consult press directories (often available at your local library) to be sure you have included all possible local or specialized media and to enhance your list for national mailings.

* Use a mailing system (labels, cards, or computerized lists) which can be updated at the last minute, and which permits you to manually select certain names for special mailings.

* Code the labels for those reporters who have taken a friendly interest in your organization so that you can easily mail to them without mailing to everyone on the contact list on which they appear.

* Update your lists regularly (at least every six months). News personnel change positions and organizations frequently, and many are offended to receive mail addressed to their predecessors.

Setting priorities. Once your contact lists are prepared, refer to your promotion goals and objectives and set priorities for the types of publicity to be sought. If the public is generally unaware of your services or if your agency suffers from a negative public image, you may want to attract as much publicity as possible for all of your programs and facilities. However, you may have certain events or new or underutilized facilities and programs toward which you want to attract special media attention.

Press releases. Press releases are short descriptions of news from your organization, prepared in a specialized format which imitates newspaper writing. The lead paragraph is the most important part of the release. It summarizes two or three of "the five Ws" in your story--the who, what, where, why and when. Editors will decide whether your release is important enough to follow-up largely on the basis of this lead paragraph. If a newspaper prints only the first paragraph due to space limitations, it is essential that it includes all of the most important information about your story. The second paragraph answers any of the "five Ws" not covered in the lead, and any subsequent paragraphs should include progressively less-important information. Provide a headline which briefly summarizes the most important points of your article. The editor may change the headline, but you should use your headline to catch that person's interest.

Your press release should be one page, or shorter, if possible. A second page is acceptable for a very important story. It should be typed on letterhead, preferably with your logo. Some organizations have special stationery printed for press releases saying, "News From ...." Indicate the date and time that the news is to be released. Either state that the release is effective immediately, or in the case of a story breaking at a preset time (like a news conference), indicate the precise time for its release (such as 10 A.M., July 17). Always have an organization contact person listed at the top of your release, and make sure that person is available to answer questions. If your contact is not available when a reporter calls, your story probably will not be printed. Carefully select which of the people on your contact lists should receive the release.

Here are some additional helpful hints:

* Use colored envelopes and/or a logo on your envelopes to grab the editor's attention.

* Include a handwritten note if you have talked to the editor or reporter.

* Tie your story to an action or event ("Parks Director takes Mayor to see deteriorating park" is an action, whereas "city park is deteriorating" is not).

* Do not overlook human-interest feature stories. This will considerably increase your chances of getting coverage. They account for about half of the available space in most papers and much of the programming on electronic media. The stories are also generally friendlier and longer than straight news stories. However, feature stories are also difficult to control. You may offer a reporter a great deal of your time and the time of others in your organization, at great inconvenience, only to discover that the story is not used or that it is mildly critical of your organization. Remember to exercise care in what you say before the story is complete, because nothing is ever really "off the record."

* Give a local or perhaps a national angle. Why is this story important in your locale? or to the nation?

* Give evidence to support your lead (include statistics, etc.) and give examples of what you are saying (Oak Park is an example of a city park which is deteriorating due to a lack of adequate funding for maintenance").

* Never state an opinion in a press release unless it is a quotation, and never include quotes without

attribution (who said it, and their position in the organization).

* Indicate what action the readers can take, including who they can contact for more information.

* Give information on what your organization's major efforts are (in the last paragraph, usually).

* Include a listing of other organizations or individuals who support you or your positions.

* Looks are important! Never use mimeograph or carbon--a good photocopy or instant-printing is acceptable. Double space and do not type the entire release in "caps." Provide adequate margins.

* "30" is the traditional way to end a press release. Other alternatives are "end" or "#####."

Building rapport with the media. Shipping out press releases to those persons on your comprehensive contact list appears to be a complete, systematic approach to gaining publicity, but there is more that you can do to enhance your chances for positive publicity. Build and nurture relationships with reporters, editors, and producers. Come to understand their needs and provide them with the types of stories that will appeal to their audiences in a form that they can readily use.

Target key media people to receive personal follow-up visits or phone calls. This will give you an opportunity to make a direct pitch for your story. Choosing who to target is an important step which should not be taken lightly. A little detective work may be needed to determine who can do something about getting your story printed or aired and who is likely to be most receptive and friendly to you and your story.

Be well-prepared when you contact the media. Have a fact-sheet available to aid you in responding to any questions. To "sell" your story you must first of all convince your media contact that your story is newsworthy. Show that it has enough of the following attributes: it is timely; has consequence either in being directly important to a large number of people or gravely important to a few; is controversial; involves conflict; is new; involves famous people; is novel, weird, different, mysterious, o   any; is going to change the future; has human interest (in. ve ove, hate, tragedy, sex, children, or animals); has suspense or adventure; will help the reader earn more money, enjoy better health, or live longer; and relates to a "hot" news item.

Secondly, you must indicate that your story would be ideal for their particular format. Show that it would be a good story for their thirty-second taped interview if that is their format, or for their half-hour discussion if that is their approach.

Thirdly, you need to prove that your story would be interesting to their audiences.

Lastly, you must let them know that you will provide intelligent, interesting spokespersons. Call well before their deadline and be brief. Expect to complete your conversation in two minutes or less. Identify yourself and your organization, and state why they will be interested in your story. Remind them of any appropriate dates, times, or special problems. Ask whether they need more information, and whether you should call back later for a response. Offer to send any written materials, including bios, press releases, or press packets.

Here are some more tips for building rapport with the media:

* Watch television, read all the newspapers, and listen to the radio. You will learn the kinds of stories they use, and who they are interested in interviewing. Then you can match your stories to their interests. Involve others on your staff in this assessment, and pool their observations.

* Contact local television and radio public-affairs directors to determine the kinds of public-affairs programming they are offering and which programs might have a format conducive to publicizing your agency and its programs and facilities. Then contact the producers of promising programs with well-thought-out proposals for future broadcasts.

* Do not approach reporters with stories that they can never use. Don't send a park closure story to the entertainment editor.

* Be aware of their deadlines. Give them as much lead-time as possible.

* Be available for questions and for supplying additional information. You are the reporter's link to the facts about your stories. If they need more facts at deadline time, you must get them what they need expeditiously.

* Be very polite and friendly. Start with first and last names, and try to get on a first-name basis.

* Control your emotions. Even when you are furious at a story that misrepresents your organization, try to maintain good relations with the media in order to protect your chances of getting better coverage in the future. In some cases expressing anger at a story may yield positive results, but generally the best policy is to thank the reporter for the parts of the story they got right and offer corrections for the parts they missed. Give them the benefit of the doubt--the final result may have been their editor's fault. Calmly ask for a follow-up story correcting the inaccuracies or mistaken impressions conveyed by the original story. However, if a reporter's coverage is consistently inaccurate or unfair, it is time to alert their editor to the problem. In relaying your concerns to the editor, stress that you value their continued coverage and are asking only that the editor closely monitor any subsequent stories concerning your agency that are prepared by that reporter.

* Be careful what you say. Nothing is really ever off the record.

* Be devastatingly accurate. Never, ever lie or make unfounded allegations or personal slanders. Always have facts at hand to back-up what you say. Be consistent with your statements and your responses to questions. Prepare your spokespersons for hostile or difficult questions to assure that their statements do not contradict each other and that they are consistent with your organization's overall goals and objectives.

* Express your thanks whenever you can. Thank the reporter for a well-done article. Thank a television producer for an interview you liked. Let a radio reporter know if their report brought you good results. Also, write letters to their supervisors complimenting the professional job that was done.

<u>Ascertainments: interviews by station management</u>. Consider doing an ascertainment. Current Federal Communications Commission rules require all radio and TV station executives to conduct interviews with "significant individuals and groups" in the community to "ascertain" what problems the community

YOU ARE BOMBARDED WITH HUNDREDS OF ADVERTISEMENTS EVERY DAY.

has and whether community interests are being aired. Station
executives must interview many individuals each month to meet
their quotas.

An ascertainment interview could take fifteen minutes, and you
can use the opportunity to make a brief presentation about your
organization at the same time. Be prepared to state what you
feel are the most significant problems in the community,
while the executives complete a brief questionnaire. As an
alternative, you could invite station executives to do ascertainments with your organization staff or volunteers in order to
introduce the media to your organization. Or you might arrange
to provide ascertainments with the local public-affairs
directors association, which could visit your organization en
masse. You might also want to examine the station's ascertainment files to determine what your community's "top 10" problems
are. By preparing a public service announcement that responds
to one of the "top 10," you may increase your chances of
getting air-time. The following chapter on advertising
includes a discussion on how to prepare an effective public
service announcement (page   ).

ADVERTISING

"Plop, plop, fizz, fizz"--you know what advertising is. You
are bombarded with hundreds of advertisements every day.
Advertising is media communication in which the sponsor is
identified. Unlike publicity, there is usually a fee for
advertising, although it is sometimes waived, as in the case
of public service announcements. Common media used in
advertising are newspapers, radio, television, outdoor billboards, posters, transit signs, magazines, shopping guides,
the telephone yellow pages, theater screens, direct mail,
leaflets, and recreation program schedule brochures.

Setting priorities. Refer again to your promotion goals and
objectives and set priorities on the types of advertising
to be produced. Advertising offers many of the same features
as publicity, but it is more controllable. You can carefully
plan an advertising campaign aimed at informing the public
about targeted programs, facilities, or events; or you can
direct your advertising toward improving or highlighting the
image of your agency.

Beware of advertising a facility or program of questionable
quality. Advertising cannot sell a poorly delivered service
more than once. By encouraging use of a service before its

deficiencies are remedied, you will make it harder to build a favorable reputation even after the problems have been ironed out.

Media selection. Media selection is a two-step process. First, intermedia comparisons should be made to determine which broad classes of media (newspapers, radio, television, etc.) should be used to meet your priority advertising objectives. Next, intramedia comparisons should be made to identify the best media choices within each of the broad classes selected. For example, if radio is the media type selected, the radio stations received in your area should then be compared to determine which are to be used in your advertising campaign.

The objective of the media selection process is to match your target audience with the most cost-effective media combination that will successfully reach them. There are five major factors to consider in making this judgment:

1. REACH--The number of persons exposed to the advertising messages through the medium.

2. FREQUENCY--The number of times a person is exposed to the advertising messages through the medium.

3. DELIVERY--The ability of the medium to expose people at a time and place at which they are receptive to the message.

4. SELECTIVITY--The ability of the medium to target a desired audience for exposure to the message.

5. EFFICIENCY--The ability to provide reach, frequency, delivery, and selectivity at the lowest possible price.

The main consideration in the media selection process is usually the REACH a medium has. A medium's reach can be discussed not only in terms of the total number of people exposed, but also in terms of the number possessing particular socio-economic characteristics or residing in a particular geographic area. All media sales representatives have plenty of demographic and survey information on the reach of their communication vehicle.

An adequate FREQUENCY assures that not only is the target audience exposed to the message, but that they are reminded of the message enough times that they overcome their inertia and act on the message.

In some situations, DELIVERY or SELECTIVITY can be extremely significant factors. The circumstances of delivery are particularly important when the message is complicated and requires the full attention of the audience. Selectivity can be the overriding factor if you need to reach a very specific clientele.

EFFICIENCY is also very important. However, if a particular medium is not capable of reaching a large enough audience to effectively broadcast your message, it will not fully satisfy your communication needs regardless of how efficient it is. If this is the case, consider using it in conjunction with another medium with a larger reach.

"Cost-per-thousand" (CPM) is the cost of reaching one thousand things, whether it be households, women, children between the ages of 9-16, or residents within the city limits. It is the most commonly used means of comparing relative intra-media cost efficiency. Ideally, figures for the cost of reaching one thousand members of your target audience should be obtained from media sales representatives and/or the Standard Rate and Data Service that publishes media rate books for all major media (check your public library). Unfortunately, there may be no statistics on how many of your target audience are reached by the media options being evaluated, especially if you have targeted a segment of the population not commonly targeted in advertising campaigns. When such statistics are unavailable, you may have to refer to more-general figures, such as the cost per thousand circulation in the case of print media or the cost per thousand homes reached in the case of broadcast media.

Intermedia cost efficiency comparisons are even more difficult to quantify. Attempting to compare the cost of reaching one thousand readers, viewers, or listeners brings to mind the often-heard warning against comparing apples and oranges. The impact of viewing your message on television will be quite different than the effect of reading it in a newspaper or magazine or hearing it on the radio. Each type of media has its own strengths and weaknesses. These attributes are often more suited to qualitative comparison than quantitative analysis. The Media Attributes Section to follow will help you make these intermedia comparisons.

Just as there is no easy formula for determining which type of media to use, there is also no easy formula for determining the optimum frequency and timing for running your advertisements. There are two basic axioms, however, that provide some general guidance: (1) people forget quickly and (2) repetition aids retention. These basic observations of human nature suggest that if your advertising budget is limited, you shouldn't try to obtain a reach that is too broad at the expense of frequency, or your message will soon be forgotten.

One technique for stretching an advertising budget is "flighting," which is the concentration of advertising into bursts with a hiatus of no advertising in between. Another is "pulsing," which is continuous advertising plus periodic bursts that reflect seasonal changes, special promotions, and other such considerations.

<u>Media attributes</u>. As mentioned earlier, there are several media commonly used in advertising park and recreation programs.

NEWSPAPERS are broad-reach local advertising media ideal for meeting many of your agency's advertising needs. People of all ages, both sexes, every educational and income level, and varied cultural and recreational interests read newspapers. And surveys have shown conclusively that the advertising is read as much as the news content of newspapers.

Newspapers allow for in-depth examination of your advertisement--readers can absorb and comprehend your advertising message. They can even clip it and refer to it when they are in a position to respond to it. Newspapers provide you with intensive coverage in a well-defined region, and they are timely and flexible. Your advertisements can be placed and withdrawn on short notice and changed quickly and frequently.

Don't overlook special newspaper sections or editions as a means to reach target audiences, and look into Sunday supplements to attract those looking for something to do on a Sunday afternoon. Sunday is by far the favorite day of the week for newspaper reading, and in one-newspaper towns and cities, Sunday supplements reach 90% of all readers.

RADIO is generally considered to be a low-cost, low-reach medium with the ability to provide high frequency and selectivity very efficiently. It is often used as a complementary medium, supporting messages conveyed in other media which have larger reach. Radio stations tend to enjoy intense listener loyalty and often attract a distinct clientele with definable age and other socio-economic characteristics. If you need to reach a very specific target audience, radio is likely to be a good choice.

The voice of a radio announcer can offer a sense of immediacy and excitement to the message, and when used creatively, radio advertising can stimulate imaginative visual pictures. Radio does not always retain the full attention of its audience, since it permits the listener to do other things while listening. However, this medium is often successful in blending its commercial messages with its program content. This makes it less likely that the audience will "tune-out" your message.

Radio is timely and flexible, allowing changes in copy on short notice. Although 80% of all radio spots are 60 seconds long, 30-second and 10-second spots may also be available.

TELEVISION offers you maximum reach. The average home spends over six hours a day watching television--an astonishing figure that keeps growing year after year. Television advertising is also usually extremely expensive and not very selective. This inefficiency can be controlled somewhat through judicious placement of commercials in programming likely to attract your target audience. However, since television stations often reach a geographic area much wider than that serviced by a local park and recreation department, it is generally an inefficient media for conveying local park and recreation information. Advertising on cable and UHF television is usually less expensive than on VHF television, but may or may not prove to be more efficient. Public service announcements, free speech messages, and community calendars represent potential free television advertising opportunities which should also be investigated.

In offering sight, sound, and motion, television provides an opportunity to physically demonstrate your programs and facilities in a way not possible with other media. Television also comes closer than any of the other mass media to duplicating the impact of personal contact. The "face-to-face" contact offered by the television medium can encourage a feeling of trust and create an aura of believability. But perhaps television advertisers have leaned on this tendency too hard. A survey conducted by the Opinion Research Corporation for the Newspaper Advertising Bureau found that only 34% of those surveyed said television advertising was either "very believable" or "believable" compared with 68% for newspapers, 59% for radio, 52% for magazines, and 25% for direct mail.

Television spots can run anywhere from 10 to 60 seconds, or even several minutes in the case of political advertising. However, 70% of television spots run 30 seconds.

BILLBOARDS reach people on the street, in cars, and on mass transit. They are relatively inexpensive and are quite effective in creating a memorable impression and reinforcing it through repetition. However, since people view billboards for only a few seconds, the messages must be simple and swift.

A number of billboards are generally required in various locations in your service area to reach a large percentage of your potential users. But in cases where your target audience is known to congregate in or pass by a certain location, one strategically placed billboard might provide highly selective, efficient reach.

However, billboards sometimes degrade the scenic values of an area, and in such cases may be considered an inappropriate medium for park and recreation advertising.

POSTERS are often placed in retail store windows or on bulletin boards as an inexpensive means of communicating with the public. The success of poster advertising hinges on locating them in prominent locations at eye level. Posters are especially effective when placed in a location where they can be read by people who are waiting for something or somebody, such as in a laundromat, at a bus stop, in line for a movie, or at a grocery checkout stand.

Flashy banners strung over Main Street and the front of City Hall have proven to be an extremely effective kind of poster for promoting upcoming special events. Banners have also been used successfully to announce deadlines for recreation program registration.

TRANSIT SIGNS are generally a moderate-cost advertising medium, although the rates vary from city to city depending on the average monthly ridership and the number of buses or subway cars which carry your ad. You can obtain extremely broad coverage using transit signs if you are located in an urban area. Almost every major artery in every major city is covered by a bus route.

There are two kinds of transit signs: interior and exterior. Interior signs in buses and subways offer long exposure to a captive audience who often have time on their hands and are thus receptive to reading your message. The challenge is to create an advertisement that stands out from the others on display. Quality graphics, striking visuals, and stimulating copy are essential. Since transit signs are often the target of vandals, determine whether it is the transit district, their contractor, or your organization that is responsible for periodically checking for problems and replacing damaged signs.

Exterior signs act like moving billboards. If you are attempting to reach residents of a particular geographic area, you can increase your selectivity and efficiency by confining your advertising to buses that run through your target neighborhoods.

MAGAZINES offer highly selective, efficient reach for a broad variety of target audiences when their circulation area matches your service area. Magazines with national circulations may not be of much use to state or local park and recreation departments, but you may want to consider advertising in local specialty magazines such as college and high school publications, seasonal sports and team programs, theater programs of summer stock or community interest, or city and regional magazines whose circulation area roughly matches or is included in your service area. Be aware, though, that advertising space in some local specialty magazines is intentionally priced above its real value and is purchased by organizations wishing to contribute to a worthy cause.

SHOPPING GUIDES are newspaper-like tabloids which carry very little or no news or editorial material. They are entirely or almost entirely filled with advertising. Nobody knows for sure why so many people leaf through pages and pages of often poorly printed advertising week after week, but there has recently been a phenomenal rise in shopping guides. Some attribute it to the "attic instinct" in many of us.

Circulation figures for shopping guides which are leafletted or mailed to "occupant" are not comparable to circulation figures for media which are solicited by their recipients. Unsolicited shopping guides are more likely to end up in the trash unread. However, when people open a shopping guide, they know very well that they are going to be exposed to a paper full of advertisements for goods and services, and as a result, shopping guide readers are less likely than newspaper or magazine readers to skip over your advertisement to get to the editorial content.

TELEPHONE YELLOW PAGES are an easy way to communicate your location to the public. Recreation facilities with a telephone (other than a pay phone) are eligible for a free line printed

in regular type in the yellow pages. If you want a boldface
listing, listings in more than one category, or larger display
advertisements, you will pay a fee. Many public recreation
agencies rent their facilities for private social events
like weddings, dances, and banquets. Yet few advertise this
service in the yellow pages under "Banquet Rooms" or "Halls
and Auditoriums" as the Southgate Recreation and Park District
in Sacramento has done with great success.

THEATRE SCREEN advertising offers a captive audience at rates
that are based on theater attendance and what the advertising
traffic will bear. Messages generally run from 40 to 60
seconds, and the usual life of a theatre screen advertising
contract is 13 weeks of daily showings.

DIRECT MAIL is the third largest advertising method after
television and newspapers. There are 34 billion direct mail
advertising pieces received each year in the United States,
and 80% of these are opened and read, according to the Postmaster
General's Office. Direct mail gives you the opportunity to
personalize your communication by addressing it to the
recipient and to focus special attention on your message by
isolating it from other messages.

Direct mail also offers the ultimate in selectivity by allowing you to decide precisely who is to receive your messages.
You can reach potential customers on the basis of any number
of socio-economic or geographic qualifiers such as age, sex,
special interest, or residence. You can mail to a city
block or to the entire state. Your only limits in selectivity
are the precision of the mailing lists you use.

Direct mail provides you with flexibility and control in
other ways too. You control both format and content. You
can mail short notices and reminders or more extensive
information when necessary. There are no page limitations
or lead times and no deadlines or broadcast schedules.

It is not uncommon to hear direct mail referred to as "junk
mail." This is due to the abuse of mailing lists by
unselective advertisers who blanket an area or class of people
without any consideration of whether these recipients are
actually prospects for what is being advertised. For
communicating certain general information, you may want to
mail to everyone in your service area. But if you are
planning on mailing specialized information, you should
consider using a limited mailing list.

If you want to purchase a mailing list, there are hundreds of list brokers (check the telephone yellow pages). Most lists sell for $25 to $50 per thousand names and are guaranteed accurate within 95%. This means no more than 5 pieces of mail will come back undelivered from each 100 mailed.

You can also compile your own list from many readily available sources, including registration lists from your recreation programs; reverse telephone directories with names of residents listed by street address; municipal and county records such as building permits; newspaper announcements of births, weddings, and engagements; and membership lists from health clubs, sports organizations, women's clubs, fraternal orders, and parent-teacher organizations. You may want to consider enlarging your list by exchanging names with other agencies or organizations with similar clientele.

The cost of direct mail can be high on the basis of cost per thousand reached, but the response rate is usually also extremely high. When evaluating the costs of direct mailing, consider the cost of compiling an effective mailing list, mailing costs, paper costs (envelopes and contents), and the cost of preparing the contents (including designing the format, composing the text, creating any artwork, and typing and printing the material).

First-class mail is rarely suitable for bulk mailings, because it is about twice as expensive as third-class bulk-rate mail. The advantages of first-class mail are its speed and its ability to reach those who automatically discard third-class mail unopened. You can often avoid the need to mail first class by planning your mailing well ahead of time and by disguising its third-class status. By leaving the return address blank and affixing precancelled stamps rather than printing a permit number on the envelopes, you can avoid the "junk mail" stigma. Some of the third-class bulk-rate stamps look just as respectable as a first-class stamp.

Postal fee structures are constantly changing, so contact your post office for assistance in selecting which mailing method best meets your needs. Also check to see which public and non-profit postage rates or combination of rates you are eligible for. Some park and recreation agencies have set up non-profit associations whose primary purpose is to conduct direct mailings for the agency at the lowest possible mailing rate.

One way to avoid unnecessary expense is to keep your mailing lists current by periodicially purging old names. It is not unusual for 25% of list entries to change in a single year. You should consider sending out a perforated double postcard annually asking that the recipient mail back half with their corrected name and address (guarantee postage). Also, check any lists you have bought or exchanged and weed out duplications. Another way to increase the efficiency of direct mailing is to plan to have your message arrive on a Tuesday, Wednesday, or Thursday and try to avoid having it arrive several days before or the day immediately following a holiday.

LEAFLETS offer the same control and flexibility as direct mail and also about the same costs, except that with leaflets you have the cost of hand delivery instead of postage. House-to-house delivery of leaflets can provide the same geographic selectivity as direct mailing, although it is probably more likely that a leaflet will be discarded unread than a first-class letter. Leaflets can also be distributed in less-selective ways. They can be handed out at locations frequented by large numbers of your target audience, or stacks of them can be left in stores at check-out counters, in libraries, and in other strategic places so people can help themselves.

RECREATION PROGRAM SCHEDULE BROCHURES enable recreation providers to convey detailed information about the content, location, and scheduling of all their programs. A well-prepared brochure can also serve as (a) an immediate inducement to register for recreation programs and (b) a long-term reference identifying the location of facilities, indicating the availability of drop-in programs, and providing key telephone numbers. A professional-looking brochure will have the additional effect of greatly enhancing the image of your agency or organization.

The efficiency and effectiveness of recreation program schedule brochures can vary greatly, depending largely on the means of production and distribution. Don't assume that the least-expensive mode of producing a brochure will be the most efficient. The public generally associates a high-quality brochure with high-quality programs. To be most effective, a brochure should have an eye-catching cover, an attractive format, appealing photographs depicting the activities being offered, and intriguing program/course titles and descriptions. For more information. refer to the handbook section, Preparing and Distributing Recreation Program Schedule Brochures (page 148).

Preparing an advertisement. Regardless of the media you select, the key to designing a good advertisement is to not lose sight of your advertising goals and objectives. You can create a very clever advertisement that fails miserably in conveying the desired message.

There are five fundamental steps in designing a successful advertisement. First, attract the attention of your target audience. Nobody is waiting for your advertisement to appear except you. The public is bombarded with messages constantly, so you must strive to make your communication stand out in a crowd and catch the eye of your intended audience. Whether utilizing a print medium or a broadcast medium, the first few thoughts--the headline--is the key. Of the people who see a printed advertisement, 90% read only the headline, and it is also common for those listening and viewing broadcast media to tune out after an opening that they don't identify with.

The headline should suggest that here is something the audience wants. If you have useful news, such as upcoming events, new programs or facilities, or new hours of operation, be sure to get this news into your headline. Provide a positive tenor rather than painting the gloomy, negative side of the picture.

Secondly, outline the benefits of your facilities and programs more fully in the main text. Use the consumers' viewpoint, and see the services through their eyes. People want to know what your service can do for them. Also anticipate and allay any doubts individuals may have about the event, facility, or program you are advertising.

Thirdly, provide proof or evidence substantiating these benefits. Don't overstate your case by promising more than you can deliver--understatement tends to be more convincing than overstatement anyway--but demonstrate the value of your services by providing statistics, endorsements from satisfied users and credible celebrities, or some other convincing evidence.

Next, encourage people to take advantage of your services. Bring the benefits to life. Help them envision how important the service can be for them, how great it will make them feel, and how easy it is for them to use it. Tell your location, your access to transit lines, and the availability of parking. Help them overcome the inertia that discourages people from acting even when they know it's in their own interest.

Finally, make a direct call for action--something simple, easy and specific. It is important to encourage your target audience to take immediate action, because the longer they delay in acting after receiving your communication, the less likely it is that they will take any action. If you neglect this step, you may find that although you have succeeded in convincing your target audience of the benefits of your services, they never get around to trying out your facility or program.

Some additional hints for preparing an advertisement are:

* Ask questions in the advertisement that stimulate a response in favor of your service.

* Make sure that your message conveys not only all of the essential information, but also the agency image you want.

* Consider including a phone number that can be called to obtain more information.

* Don't distract the audience with relatively unimportant information.

* Be natural and personable in your copy, and make it entertaining to read, watch, or listen to your advertisement.

* Don't talk down to your audience, but keep the complexity of your pitch at a level readily understandable by the average person.

* Use short, simple sentence construction and vocabulary.

* Use the present tense, singular instead of plural. By individually addressing your audience with the second person "you," your message will be personalized.

* Use pictorial nouns and action verbs, and where possible, avoid adjectives, dependent clauses, and the subjective mood.

* Punctuate for clarity and vigor. Good punctuation makes your copy march forward.

* Use only one typeface, in various sizes and weights, to avoid a clash of typefaces that don't look good together.

The first option may not be an effective technique in generating large sums of money to finance an extensive brochure, but it could be a good choice for agencies or organizations that are offering a relatively small number of programs and are envisioning a more modest brochure.

The effectiveness of the second option has been demonstrated by the Foothills Metropolitan Recreation and Park District near Denver, Colorado. For the last two and a half years, the District has recovered the full cost of publishing their high-quality quarterly brochure (about $13,000 for 50,000 copies) by soliciting large advertisements for the center section and back cover of their brochure.

The third option of intermixing advertisements with program information may have the greatest potential for revenue generation, but it can also reduce the readability of the brochure and its promotion value. Skillful layout design can minimize, but never completely eliminate this drawback.

Before approaching prospective sponsors, prepare an argument convincing them that sponsoring your brochure will be in their best interest. The Foothills Metropolitan Recreation and Park District conducted a telephone marketing survey documenting that the average household refers to each of their quarterly brochures 6-8 times. Armed with this information and a portfolio that they assemble for each prospective sponsor, they are ready to make a case that their brochure is a good advertising opportunity.

Recruting sponsors for your brochure can sometimes be a very time-consuming task, depending on the size of your community and the amount of money to be raised. The cities of Anaheim and Newport Beach in California have found a way to obtain advertising revenue without this expenditure of staff time. They contract with advertising agencies to print and mail their brochures in return for the right to sell advertising space in the brochures. The cities retain veto power over the design and content of the brochures and set a limit on the amount of advertising space the brochures can contain.

There is more than one way to assemble the political support and funding necessary to produce and distribute a quality brochure. The Department of Leisure Services for the City of Walnut Creek, California, has joined forces with the Department of Civic Arts and City Hall to produce an extremely impressive quarterly brochure, "City Scene." It is divided into three sections. One describes the programs being offered by the Department of Leisure Services, another

depicts those offered by the Department of Civic Arts, and
the center section is reserved for the Mayor and City Council
to enable them to communicate regularly with the citizenry.
The cost of printing 48,000 copies is about $12,000, which is
shared by the three offices on the basis of the number of
pages devoted to each section.

COORDINATION is important, since the preparation of recreation
program schedule brochures can require the timely input of
several staff members. Producing a top-notch brochure often
requires a carefully conceived work schedule, complete with
deadlines for the submittal of information. Everyone
responsible for providing information should be apprised of
their deadlines and should be instructed to view their input
as a high-priority cyclic task, similar in nature to the
provision of budget information. Whomever is assigned the
coordination responsibility must be isolated from competing
responsibilities during critical time periods. Some agencies
have found it difficult to effectively free anyone from their
other responsibilities and have contracted out for someone
to perform this coordination function.

KEY COMPONENTS of the brochure must be considered. The
importance of your brochure's cover as one key component can
not be stressed enough. It can make or break the effectiveness of your brochure. If you spend a little extra time and
money designing and producing an attractive cover for your
brochure, its recipients will be more apt to keep it around
their residence for awhile until they have the time and
inclination to read through it. On the other hand, if it
looks like a standard bulk-rate advertising flyer, they are
likely to quickly toss it unless they have time to read it
immediately upon receiving it.

The cover for Walnut Creek's "City Scene" is extremely
effective. It is composed of a standard title block printed
in color, which overlays a full-page block-and-white photo-
graph. The repetition of a standard title block helps the
recipient to immediately recognize it, while featuring a
different color and a different photo each issue adds variety
and sparks interest.

The City of Anaheim also places a great deal of importance
on the cover of its brochure by going to the extra expense
of printing a bright, colorful cover on glossy paper rather
than the newsprint used for the rest of the brochure. The
glossy cover quickly distinguishes the brochure from junk
mail and increases the chances that it will be retained
and read.

* Generally avoid printing in reverse type (light type on a dark background). It may look attractive, but it is more difficult to read and will tend to reduce the size of your audience.

* Use photographs in your print advertising. They increase recall substantially.

* Put captions under your photographs. Readership of picture captions is generally twice as great as body copy.

* In preparing direct mail advertising, use single-spacing, with no paragraphs longer than seven lines and with an occasional one- or two-line paragraph to break the letter up into easily readable blocks. This will give the reader a psychological boost, encouraging them to read the letter in its entirety.

* Include a p.s. in your direct mail advertising that sums up your most important message and encourages the reader to take action. Everyone reads the p.s., even if they don't read the letter all the way through.

<u>Preparing and distributing recreation program schedule brochures</u>. Some important aspects of the preparation and distribution of recreation program schedule brochures should be considered in enhancing the effectiveness of the brochures.

OUTSIDE ASSISTANCE in varying degrees, is available for preparation of these brochures. Many agencies and organizations prepare the text and the graphics, and contract out the layout and printing. This usually results in a more impressive, professional-looking brochure than what can be produced without outside help.

Producing and distributing a high-class brochure that will generate community interest can be fairly expensive, but you can reduce or completely eliminate your costs by convincing community merchants to sponsor the production and distribution of your brochure. Options include:

1. Devoting a prominent page to a listing of merchants who have donated money toward the brochure.

2. Including an insert of advertisements and/or discount coupons.

3. Selling advertising space throughout the brochure.

The importance of an attractive format with intriguing program/course titles and descriptions is self-evident. Which of these course descriptions would be more likely to attract your interest? This one?

ITALIAN COOKING

Learn to cook several kinds of homemade pasta and sauces.

Or this one found in the "Fall Festival of Activities" put out by the City of Santa Cruz, California?

PASTA CRAZY

Pasta lovers unite! Learn to color it green, yellow and red, sauce it Alfredo, seal it into ravioli, toss it with pesto. Discover the joys of fresh, homemade pasta and its infinite varieties.

A carefully selected picture may very well be worth a thousand words. Walnut Creek's brochure is full of quality photographs graphically depicting their programs and facilities and showing participants who are thoroughly enjoying themselves. For potential participants who just need a little encouragement, these photos can be extremely persuasive. The selection of subjects for the photos is made by a graphics expert in consultation with each department head. Volunteer photographers are then recruited from the department's photography classes to take the photos, with the city covering the costs of their photographic supplies.

DISTRIBUTION TECHNIQUES can also impact the effectiveness of your brochures. The distribution can be handled by direct mail (which is probably the most effective method, but can also be quite expensive) or through the mechanisms described in the section on leaflets (page 143).

The Anaheim Park and Recreation Department has cut the cost of direct mailing substantially by setting up a non-profit corporation that distributes their brochures at the non-profit postage rate, which is quite a bit lower than the rate charged to cities. The current (1982) basic presort bulk-mailing rate is 10.9¢ for governmental agencies and 4.9¢ for authorized non-profit organizations. The cost for 200 or more pieces that are presorted by five-digit zip code is 9.3¢ for governmental agencies and 4¢ for authorized non-profit organizations. The Anaheim non-profit corporation has found that they save money by contracting with a private firm to presort their mail by five-digit zip code so that they can obtain the 4¢ rate.

The Hayward Area Recreation District in the San Francisco Bay Area distributes its recreation program schedule information as an insert in either a daily newspaper or a shopping guide, whichever offers the lowest bid. Using this method, 65,000 copies are distributed as inserts, and another 5,000 copies are distributed through various other channels by the recreation district. A newspaper or shopping guide insert is a relatively inexpensive method of distribution, but it will not reach as many people as direct mailing or hand delivery.

The Foothills Metropolitan Recreation and Park District contracts with a private company to hand-deliver their brochures door-to-door for 5.5¢ each. Some argue that brochures are more apt to be tossed if they are left in a plastic bag attached to the doorknob than if they arrive in the mail. However, if it is a high-quality brochure with a professional-looking cover, this may not be the case. One advantage to hand-delivery is that you can assure that all of your brochures will be delivered in a timely manner, whereas the exact time of bulk mail delivery cannot be assured.

Another common method of distribution is to hand out brochures to school children. Each child is given a brochure to take home for the use of his or her family. This method will fail to reach large segments of the population, including most single adults, most senior citizens, and the growing number of couples without children. Some agencies and organizations use this technique as a supplement to other distribution mechanisms.

<u>Free assistance</u>. This handbook provides you with basic tools and techniques to help you develop successful advertising programs, but it is certainly desirable to obtain as much assistance as possible from professional advertising specialists who have the benefit of extensive training and years of experience. If hiring such help is beyond the reach of your budget, you should consider seeking a specialist willing to volunteer his or her time. The field of parks and recreation has an inherent ability to attract people's interest and hold their attention, providing many opportunities for entertaining messages. Advertising specialists who have been struggling to make a client's mundane products seem exciting may welcome the opportunity to develop an advertising campaign for a park and recreation agency. Such volunteer

work can serve to stimulate their creative juices, generate favorable publicity for them and their agencies, and provide them with a sense of fulfillment in having contributed to the welfare of their community.

One source of free help is the Advertising Council, which is supported entirely by the advertising-communications industry and American business. However, they only work on campaigns which promote voluntary citizen actions to help solve problems that are national in scope. There are also a growing number of local non-profit advertising federations and professional associations. They are composed of local advertising, graphics, and other private professionals who pool their resources to assist local causes as a free service.

Free advertising information and assistance are also available from a variety of other sources. Check with state recreation associations, the National Recreation and Park Association, media sales representatives, and the various advertising bureaus (Newspaper Advertising Bureau, Inc., Radio Advertising Bureau, Inc., Transient Advertising Bureau, Inc., and Television Advertising Bureau, Inc.).

When you purchase a newspaper advertisement, preparation of the advertisement is free, from the first word of copy to the last illustration, as long as you are willing to settle for what their advertising department offers. Most newspaper offer complete layout and finished copy, combining the artwork they buy from artwork services with some simple handwork such as line sketches. They generally will not take special photographs for you but will work with your photographs-- cropping, fitting, and integrating them into your advertisement. The advertising professionals know their business better than anyone else, but stay involved and actively monitor them to increase your chances of getting creative, rather than canned, advertising.

Negotiation is often utilized in the advertising business. You might suggest to advertising representatives that your organization would like to try out their channel free or at a reduced rate with the possibility of future commissions. Don't be shy. The worst they can say is "no." Remember that unless you ask, your chances of getting donated advertising is slim.

Public agencies and nonprofit recreation organizations throughout the country receive free advertising on radio, television, and outdoor billboards donated as a public service. Each June, the _Miami Herald_ donates an entire page of advertising space to the public recreation agency in Dade County to celebrate National Recreation and Parks Month.

Promotion of recreation programs in Natick, Massachusetts, costs the taxpayers very little. Local merchants sponsor advertisements which pay the cost of producing the town's recreation program brochure. The merchants also distribute the brochures in their places of business. Cooperation with local public school officials has led to an arrangement whereby the brochures are distributed at school to all students in grades 1-12, who then take the brochures home to their families.

In Newport Beach, California, the Department of Parks, Beaches, and Arts turned over production and distribution of its program brochure to a private advertising firm. In return for revenues from advertising space, the firm designed, printed, and distributed a brochure of superior quality at a substantial cost saving to the city. The city retained quality control through absolute veto power on the nature, content, and amount of advertising. This arrangement has since been tried by other southern California recreation agencies.

Public-service billboards are often available for the asking at certain slack periods in the outdoor advertising cycle. The "Friends of the Zoo" in San Francisco received $30,000 worth of backlit billboard space from a large outdoor advertising firm. As a public service, the Friends were given use of dozens of billboards for a one-year period. The free advertising for the Adopt-An-Animal program resulted in over $100,000 in new memberships. The outdoor advertising firm received a tax write-off and promoted their new backlit billboards, which were subsequently leased for paid advertising.

Public-service announcements. A great deal of free air-time is donated by radio and television stations to nonprofit groups, community-service organizations, and governmental agencies to allow them to broadcast non-commercial messages called public-service announcements (PSAs). Free air-time is not something to be overlooked, but don't rely on PSAs to meet all of your advertising needs. The time of day that they are aired is determined by the broadcasting station, and it is often during non-prime-time hours when there is a relatively small audience.

Public-service announcements are generally most effective if they are well-produced, with music, slides, or film. But if you do not have the time or budget to create an elaborate public-service announcement, a well-written 30-second PSA to be read aloud by a station announcer may be extremely effective.

Local television and radio stations frequently select nonprofit agencies for station-produced PSAs. You must negotiate for these with each station's public-affairs director. These may take several months to come to fruition, but stations can produce excellent PSAs, and the station develops a special interest in getting them aired. Another source of inexpensive PSAs is local film schools, where they will often produce films for you for the cost of materials as a learning opportunity for the students.

You should never mail a PSA to a station without making personal contact first. Make an appointment with the person in charge of public-service announcements if possible. If you cannot get an appointment, try dropping by the station and asking the receptionist to let you see the person in charge of PSAs. If the date your PSA is aired is important, make sure to allow enough lead time for discussions and changes by the station.

In preparing a PSA script, include your organization's name, address, and phone number; a contact name and phone number; the number of seconds the announcement will run (10, 15, 20, or 30 seconds--only rarely do stations use 60-second PSAs); the start-date when you want the PSA to begin running; and the end-date when you want the PSA to be withdrawn from the air.

The script should be 25-150 words in length, and should mention the name of your organization at least twice.

Say you are going to ask your audience to do something; then ask them to do something; and then say that you have asked them to do something. Determine the one most important thing you want to communicate and state that idea as directly as possible, using short action verbs.

If you want people to write you or call you, repeat the address or phone number, and keep your phone number of address as simple as possible. A post office box number helps. In many cities, you can qualify for a catchword or name-box at the post office (For example, write RECREATION, San Francisco, CA 94109). Contact your post office for availability and cost.

Federal rules and regulations regarding PSAs are presently being reviewed and revised by the Federal Communications Commission, so before preparing a PSA, check with the FCC and local television and radio stations to obtain up-to-date information and instructions.

Evaluation. The final step in the effective use of advertising is advertising evaluation. Unfortunately, there is no evaluation technique which provides a precise measurement of the effectiveness of your advertising, but techniques such as copy testing, media testing, and expenditure-level testing can assist you in identifying changes which should be made in your advertising campaign.

COPY TESTING can be conducted both before and after an advertisement is printed or broadcasted. Most major advertisers go through a pretest before they commit a large amount of funds to advertising. Two methods of advertisement pre-testing are direct ratings and portfolio tests.

In utilizing the direct ratings method, a panel of individuals selected from your target audience or a panel of advertising experts examine alternative advertisements and fill out rating questionnaires. Sometimes the panel is asked only to select which advertisement would influence them most to utilize the service or facility being advertised. If a more specific evaluation is desired, the panel may be asked to evaluate the advertisement's strengths and weaknesses. For example, they might be asked:

1. How well the advertisement caught the panel's attention.

2. How well it kept the panel's attention to the end of the advertisement.

3. How clear the central message was.

4. How effective the advertisement's particular appeal was among the variety of possible appeals in arousing the desired images and emotions.

5. How successful the advertisement was in suggesting a follow-through action and motivating the panel to take action.

If an advertisement scores low in any of these areas, it may need further work.

The portfolio test is a pre-testing method in which members of the target audience are given a portfolio of advertisements and are asked to take as much time as they want to read them. After putting them down, each participant is asked to recall the advertisements they saw (sometimes aided and sometimes unaided by the interviewer) and to recollect as much as they can about each advertisement. This test demonstrates an advertisement's ability to convey its intended message and to stand out when surrounded by other media messages.

There are also two popular post-testing methods: recall tests and recognition tests. Recall tests involve finding persons who are regular users of the media vehicle and asking them to recall your advertisement in much the same way as described for the portfolio pre-test. Recall tests indicate how effective the advertisement has been in attracting attention and in being retained.

Recognition tests sample the audience of the particular broadcast or issue of a publication that contained your advertisement. Those sampled are exposed once again to the advertisement and are asked to point out what they recognize. Two statistics which are often gathered are the percentage who say they remember having been exposed to the advertisement, and the percentage who say they remember any part of the advertisement that clearly indicates the service being advertised. In the case of an advertisement in a print medium, the percentage of readers who not only looked at the advertisement, but also say that they read more than half of the total written material in the advertisement, may be another important statistic.

MEDIA TESTING is a means of evaluating which of the media utilized proved to be cost effective in reaching and influencing the target audience. One common way to test the effectiveness of a print medium is to place a coupon advertisement and see how many are returned. Similarly, the effectiveness of radio or television can be measured by making a special offer to those who can repeat a key phrase when they come to utilize your service.

EXPENDITURE-LEVEL TESTING involves arranging experiments in which expenditure levels are varied over similar market areas to see the variation in response. If the response to your advertisement is only slightly higher in the high expenditure area, you may decide that the lower budget is adequate.

PERSONAL CONTACT

The personal nature of direct interaction with the public makes it extremely effective in either building or damaging the image of your agency and its programs and facilities. Personal contact often provides an opportunity to accomplish one or more of the following three functions: (a) serving the public by welcoming them and assisting them to fully enjoy and benefit from participating in your programs and utilizing your facilities; (b) informing, reminding, or convincing the public of the benefits they can receive by utilizing your services; and (c) monitoring the effectiveness of your services by receiving feedback from users and non-users. If any of these functions are being neglected, you are not only missing a golden opportunity to promote your agency, but you may also be generating ill-will which will make future promotional efforts much more difficult.

On-site personal contact. All members of your park and recreation staff need training and guidance in user relations, including maintenance crews, security personnel, playground leaders, guides, entry attendants, and concessionaires. Their appearance, their attitude to users and other staff members, and their approach to dealing with complaints, requests, and emergencies can be critical in determining how the public views your agency. Although taking time out to discuss how to deal with the public may seem costly, haphazard "on-the-job" training in user relations can prove much more costly in lost clients and discouraged staff.

Personal contact between the public and employees accepting reservations or working at entrance stations and information desks, booths, and windows provides a key promotion opportunity. First impressions are often lasting impressions. If a user is introduced to your facility or program in a friendly, helpful, enthusiastic manner, their attitude toward it is more likely to be positive.

Many theme parks have created a specialized terminology as a constant reminder to their staffs that their role is to serve the users. They use terms like onstage, backstage, park guest, host, and hostess, which all imply positive service that is both hospitable and personal. Adopting similar terminology for your agency could prove effective in reinforcing attitudes of helpfulness in your employees.

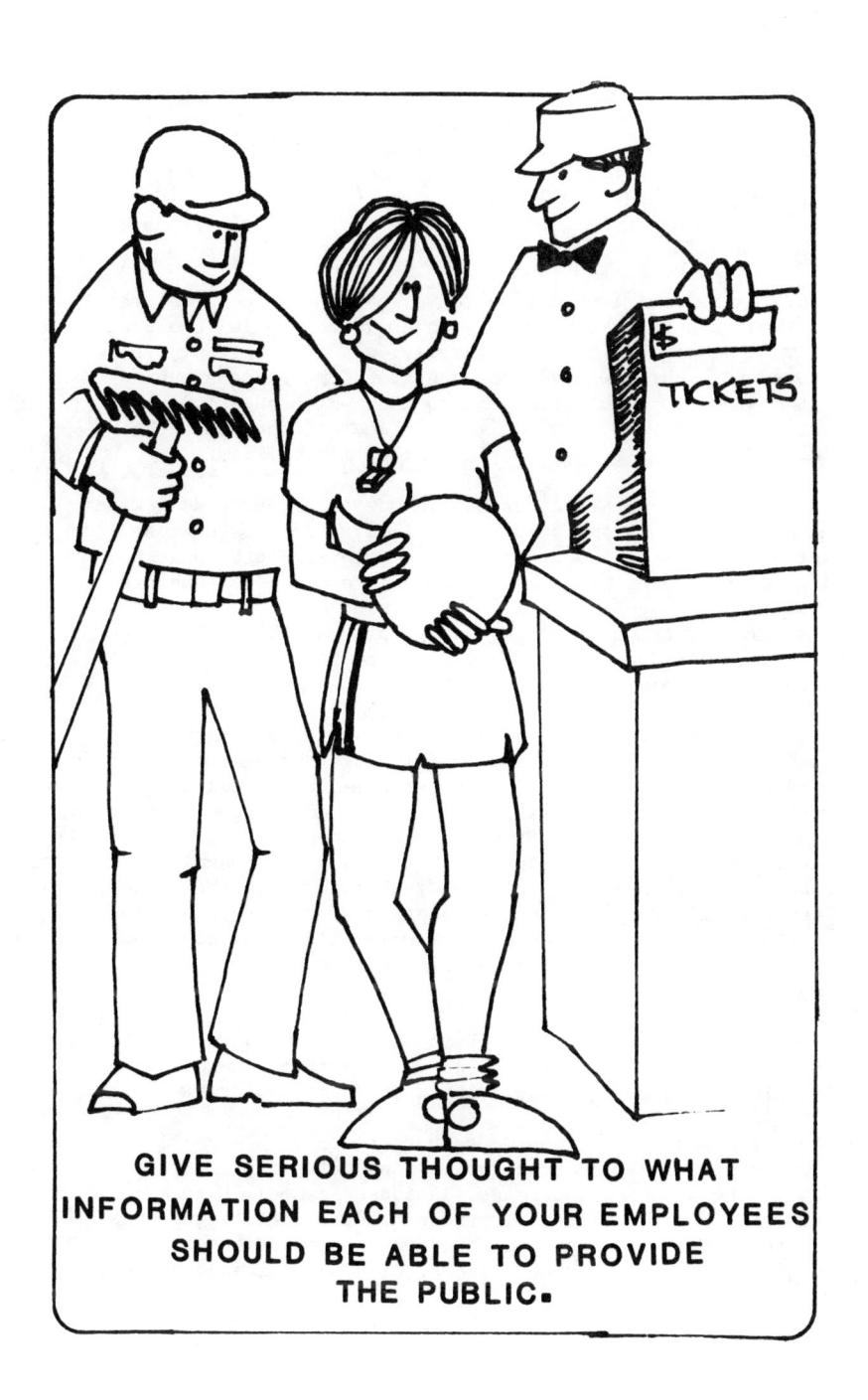

GIVE SERIOUS THOUGHT TO WHAT INFORMATION EACH OF YOUR EMPLOYEES SHOULD BE ABLE TO PROVIDE THE PUBLIC.

A helpful attitude, however, is not always sufficient in itself to assure positive user relations. Your employees must be well-informed so that they can properly assist users. Give serious thought to what information each of your agency's employees should be able to provide the public. What should your maintenance personnel be aware of? Your playground leaders? Your entry attendants?

Nothing is more frustrating to users than to feel that their actions are being confined by an employee who is interpreting a rule or regulation too literally. It is important, therefore, for your employees to understand the reasons behind the rules and regulations and to know which ones must be strictly enforced at all times and where judgment can be exercised to allow a proper amount of flexibility.

Your employees must be trained in how to properly deal with other user-relations problems as well. Identify common problem situations and train your employees to be able to effectively deal with them. There is often more than one way to successfully handle a user-relations problem, but try to demonstrate possible promising options. Then encourage discussion and utilize role playing to reinforce the techniques being discussed.

Providing an effective system for receiving user suggestions and complaints is important in allowing your agency to modify its programs and facilities to best meet the needs of the public you are serving. It is also an extremely important part of your user-relations program. Opening lines of communication in the form of suggestion boxes, complaint phone lines, or on-site personnel through which the agency consistently responds to complaints with courtesy, understanding, and action can quickly bring a halt to negative word-of-mouth advertising and can generate a positive agency image instead.

<u>Off-site personal contact</u>. Personal contact can also be used effectively off-site to provide information to the public and to receive and respond to their concerns.

One good way to gain public support is to work directly with public-service organizations and private groups, including parent-teacher associations, Jaycees, the League of Women Voters, churches, garden clubs, sport leagues and clubs, conservation groups, homeowner associations and other neighborhood organizations, professional associations, employee associations, women's clubs, and fraternal organizations such as the Lions Club, Rotary Club, and Optimist Club. These organizations are valuable not only in disseminating information, but also in sponsoring various recreation projects throughout the country.

You can obtain from the Chamber of Commerce a list of civic organizations that might be receptive to hearing about your agency's activities. If you are anxious to reach a particular target audience, select appropriate organizations and offer to speak to them. If you want to reach as many members of the community as possible, widely advertise that your agency is establishing a speakers bureau and that your agency director or some other key agency officials is available to meet with civic groups. Consider preparing a slide show to graphically illustrate your message and establish a positive image of your agency and its programs and facilities.

Another use of personal contact which can help to enhance the image of your agency is to hold community meetings or workshops to discuss planning options or to try to identify solutions to problems of wide community interest. Such gatherings can be extremely effective in gaining and sustaining community support and in generating citizen action. However, never ask for public input if a decision has already been made, or you may find that the community never responds to your call for help again.

Speaking before a group or organization gives an excellent opportunity to promote your agency and its services, but to maximize your effectiveness, prepare your remarks carefully. Your opening remarks are critical. The audience's initial impressions of you will often determine their receptivity to the substance of your message. Establish a common bond with the audience. Help them identify with you by demonstrating that you have common interests and experiences. Break down any barriers which seem to separate you. Adopt the tone of a friend and neighbor rather than a government official. If you can successfully project the image of your true likeable self and if you can exude enthusiasm about your agency's operations, you will have built a rapport with the audience and primed them to want to hear more about your services. Go beyond merely outlining the services offered. Describe the benefits that they will derive from using your facilities and participating in your programs. If you know that the audience you are addressing has certain special interests, try to relate your services to their needs. Provide illustrations, examples, testimonials, and any data you have available to demonstrate how your services can benefit them. Avoid promising something you cannot deliver or you will lose your credibility and effectiveness for future occasions. In closing, summarize the key points you want the audience to remember, and suggest to them the action you hope that they take.

Citizen advisory groups can be established as a means of obtaining more-formal feedback and input from the community. They can provide an ongoing liaison between your agency and the public. In the organizational stages of these councils, it is highly advisable that your agency set out in writing the duties, functions, and responsibilities of the committees. Conflicts can arise if it is not clear whether the citizen committee is administrative, advisory, or policy-making in nature.

Some agencies have no choice in that the functions of these bodies are written into their enabling legislation. If you do have a choice, one effective division of responsibility is to assign the committee an advisory role on basic policy matters, while retaining administrative responsibility and final policy-making authority. Under this type of organizational structure, the administration of policy is considered to be a technical problem requiring a technically trained staff. The committee's responsibility is to advise on the basic policies which guide the agency. Although the agency has no obligation to follow the recommendations of the advisory committee, the committee will soon see itself as an observer, serving no purpose, ratifying decisions already made, if the agency fails to show a general willingness to accept the committee's advice.

In organizing citizen advisory groups, try to attain representation for all age and socio-economic groups on your committee, as well as including members from throughout the agency's service area. Some of the most successful citizen committees have been organized on a neighborhood basis.

Encourage civic leaders to serve on the committee who are capable of arousing interest and stimulating constructive citizen action. Avoid those who cannot work constructively with the agency, but do not be afriad of having someone who will keep you on your toes. Continuity and the infusion of new ideas can be ensured by establishing staggered terms of office.

Committee meetings should be held at times and places which will attract the greatest attendance. An agenda is essential, but the committee should recognize its role as a liaison between the agency and the community and should provide ample opportunity for receiving input from the citizens they represent.

SPECIAL PROMOTIONS

Special promotions include such promotional techniques as offering incentives, "advertising specialties," contests, and special events. Unlike publicity, advertising, and personal contact, special promotions are generally non-routine and often non-recurring. Special promotions can be used to accomplish a wide range of objectives as discussed below. Before deciding whether to use any of these techniques as part of your promotional mix, refer to your promotional goals and objectives.

To be successful, a special promotion must be well-planned, have realistic objectives, have an adequate budget, and be designed with the target market in mind. It must also match and support your agency's image.

Conducting special promotions can be viewed by staff as being either a lot of extra work or an exciting change of pace. Consider boosting staff morale and enthusiasm about an upcoming special promotion by creating a parallel internal contest themed to the special promotion activity. For example, if you are having a recreation fair promoting your programs, you might offer prizes to the group of employees creating the most informative or most entertaining display.

<u>Incentives</u>. Incentives are defined here as something of financial value offered to encourage participation in a program or use of a facility or service. Some of the most commonly used incentives are the waiving of fees, price reductions, rebates, coupons, direct premiums, and "traffic builders." Each has its own strengths and weaknesses, so choose carefully. One or more of these incentives can be used to help meet each of the following ten objectives:

1. to encourage the sampling of existing facilities and programs;

2. to introduce a new facility or program;

3. to encourage the use of underutilized programs or facilities;

4. to level off uneven use patterns by encouraging use at non-peak times of the day, days of the week, or seasons of the year;

5. to introduce a new use for an existing facility;

6. to develop a pattern of use that carries on after the incentive has been removed;

7. to add interest and excitement to your advertising;

8. to test the effectiveness of the media you selected for your advertising;

9. to create publicity; and

10. to generate goodwill and enhance your overall agency image.

THE WAIVING OF FEES, PRICE REDUCTIONS, AND REBATES are price incentives with similar attributes. The success of price incentives is largely dependent on whether the incentive offered constitutes a significant enough savings to attract interest and whether it is adequately advertised or publicized. However, even a substantial, well-advertised savings will not be effective in promoting a poorly designed program or facility that fails to meet the needs of the community. Each of these price incentives can be used to accomplish any of the objectives listed above, with the exception of testing the effectiveness of your media advertising. The waiving of fees, often promoted as "a free introductory offer," tends to generate the most interest but is also the most expensive. Rebates are sometimes less attractive to the public because they do not offer an immediate payoff. However, they can offer the added feature of encouraging people to stay with a program until completion. For example, some agencies which offer dancing classes promise a rebate of part of the program fee if participants attend every session. This incentive can help ensure that there is an equal number of males and females present for each of the class sessions.

COUPONS are certificates with a stated value which the consumer presents to you to entitle them to a price reduction on a specified item. Coupons are often distributed door-to-door, by direct mail, or through the print media such as newspapers or magazines. They are often used to add interest and excitement to your advertising and to test the effectiveness of your advertising media. Coupons should be used carefully and selectively. If they are used to excess, the public begins to question whether your regular price truly reflects the value of your service.

"Bounceback" coupons can be used to stimulate interest in two facilities or programs at once. The "bounceback" feature means that those purchasing one product or service are given coupons entitling them to price reductions on another. For example, you could offer a coupon to those using your swimming facilities that entitles them to a reduced price at your golf course.

In designing a coupon, make sure that it looks like a coupon to be redeemed and not like an announcement of a price reduction. It should clearly tell the consumer the terms of the offer, including the facility or program involved, the value of the coupon (redemption value should be printed in bold type in at least two places on the face of the coupon), the number of services they must buy to qualify, where to redeem the coupon, and any restrictions on who qualifies for the offer.

In using coupons to evaluate the effectiveness of your advertising media, test several media mixes to see which gives the best results. Also consider comparing copy and layout options by using split-run opportunities offered by some print media, in which two different but comparable advertisements appear in alternate copies of the same edition in exactly the same position. Keep accurate records for each promotion of your redemption experience and also your use figures before, during, and after the promotion period.

DIRECT PREMIUMS AND "TRAFFIC BUILDERS" are both extras given free, directly to the consumer. The difference between the two is that in the case of a direct premium, the "gift" is given in conjunction with a purchase; whereas in the case of a "traffic builder," no purchase is necessary to obtain the "gift." Direct premiums are designed to encourage the purchase of other services that are offered. "Traffic builders" are used to encourage attendance at special events or to encourage people to visit the facility where distribution of the "gift" is occurring.

The cost of offering a direct premium is mitigated by the money derived from the purchase accompanying the premium. However, when a "traffic builder" is offered, there is no assurance that any additional revenues will result.

One way to enhance the efficiency of "traffic builders" is by offering a "gift" that appeals almost exclusively to the target group you are trying to reach. For example, if you are anxious to attract young children to a new playground facility that you have just opened or rehabilitated, you might advertise that you are going to distribute free balloons at the playground. Balloons are a good choice because they are relatively inexpensive and because, in all probability, few adults and teenagers would be attracted by the offer of free balloons. This means that most of the balloons would go to children whom you have successfully introduced to your playground, while only a few would be "wasted" on non-targeted individuals.

Another way to utilize "traffic builders" efficiently is to offer free admissions to your programs and facilities as the "gifts." Consider the playground example again. If your agency operates a zoo, you could attract children to the playground by distributing free admission tickets to the zoo, valid any day that week. Although the tickets would have a high value in the eyes of the recipients, the only cost to your agency would be potential revenue lost from those who were planning to visit the zoo anyway. You may also find that you have simultaneously promoted not only the playground, but also the zoo. Some of the recipients may begin visiting the zoo often as a result of being introduced to the experience, or some may invite friends to come along--the net result being an increase in zoo revenues.

Regardless of whether the "gift" is a direct premium or a "traffic builder," take care in selecting what to offer. It should not only be attractive to your target audience, but also consistent and supportive of your agency image. Investigate ways to avoid paying for premiums or "traffic builders." One possibility, demonstrated in the zoo example above, is to offer another agency service at a cut rate or for free. Another possibility is soliciting a direct donation. As a park and recreation agency, you may find that retailers are anxious to donate direct premiums, "traffic builders," or the money to acquire them. By so doing, they (1) obtain positive exposure for their product or business, (2) establish an association in the public's mind between recreation and their product or business, and (3) can write it all off as a business expense.

<u>Advertising specialties</u>. An "advertising specialty" is a piece of merchandise given freely, without condition, that bears an advertising imprint. Common "advertising specialties" are ball-point pens, pencils, calendars, matchbooks, and key

chains. As a public agency, the propriety of paying for an
advertising device aimed at enhancing your agency image may
well be questioned. However, you may find that there are
retailers in your community that would be more than glad to
add your agency's name and message to their advertising
specialty for no fee as a means of associating their product
with your agency.

The following considerations should be weighted in selecting
an "advertising specialty":

1. The item should be highly useful to the recipeint--
   preferably subject to repeated daily use.

2. It should be of sufficient quality and proper type
   to reflect favorably on the image of your agency.

3. It should be long-lasting.

4. It should have an imprint that not only repeatedly
   puts the name of your agency before the public, but
   also contains a message that furthers the positive
   image of the agency and/or communicates important
   information.

5. It should appeal to the target audience that you
   want to reach, and ideally to as few others as
   possible to avoid waste (although waste may not be
   an overriding consideration if someone else is
   sponsoring the item).

An example of an "advertising specialty" used by park and
recreation agencies is a tote bag imprinted with a message
asking visitors to use it to collect litter while visiting
the park, and then listing a half dozen other uses it can
be put to after leaving the area.

Contests. Sweepstakes and contests are used to create
publicity and/or to add interest to your advertising. Before
creating a sweepstake or contest, it is important that state
and federal regulations be examined. Most states carry
stipulations that prevent lotteries. A sweepstake or contest
generally becomes a lottery if it does all three of the
following: it offers a prize, demands consideration, and
includes the element of chance. So, if you plan on offering
a prize, you need to either judge the contest on the basis
of skill (with appropriate, announced judging standards) or
provide an equal opportunity for everyone to enter without
asking for any consideration in return. Requiring proof of

purchase or requiring an entrant to expend a substantial amount of time or effort to enter constitutes consideration. Other state stipulations that must be investigated include prize disclosure rules, the period for holding of all entries after the contest, regulations preventing pre-determination of winners, and possible requirements for the posting of a performance bond.

You may also want to check with the Office of the General Counsel, Mailability Division, Post Office Department, Washington, DC 20260 to make certain that your proposed contest or sweepstake is not a lottery. U.S. postal lottery laws prohibit the mailing of any newspaper, circular, pamphlet, or publication of any kind advertising a lottery regardless of whether (a) it is announcing a lottery that is legal under state law, (b) it is a paid or non-paid announcement, or (c) it gives the full story of the lottery's operation or says nothing more than "Games," "Party," or "Entertainment," or some other word or designation (for example a dollar sign) which is understood by the reader to give notice that games of chance will be played at the time and place noted. It is also illegal to mail the results of a lottery, telling who won or what prizes were awarded.

In designing a contest or sweepstake, you should select a contest theme that meets your promotional objective. The prizes must be supportive of your contest theme and attractive to your target audience. Commonly, the manufacturer of the prizes donates them in return for advertising exposure. If you are unsuccessful in obtaining large prizes, identify a set of intriguing inexpensive ones that will capture the public's imagination. Offering a spectacular grand prize may not be essential if contestants feel there are a large enough number of attractive lesser prizes to give them a reasonable chance of winning something.

State the contest rules very clearly to avoid any possible misunderstandings. Consider disallowing mechanically reproduced entries, limiting entries to one per household, and stating that all duplications will be automatically eliminated and not be given a response. An expiration date for receiving entries must also be established. Be prepared to process all entries that may be received and set specific judging standards before advertising the contest.

<u>Special events</u>. Special events often have a dual purpose. The more obvious purpose is to gather people together to have a good time, but they also can be designed to promote a specific facility or program, or to enhance the image of the

park and recreation agency sponsoring the event. By offering exciting, non-routine attractions, the agency is able to introduce or reintroduce people to a facility or activity in the hope that they will return after the event is over to make use of the featured facility or program or other agency services on an ongoing basis.

It is important that your special event relates to your overall promotion goals and objectives. There are an infinite number of possible types and formats of events. Borrow ideas from others who have sponsored successful events, but use your imagination in designing one which meets your specific needs. If one of your goals is to encourage a particular group to more fully utilize your services, design a special event that will be especially attractive to them. Consider asking this target group to help select a theme for a special event that they would like to attend and let them help you plan the event. If one of your goals is to boost attendance at an underutilized facility, consider holding a special event at the site, carefully designed not only to attract a large number of people to the facility, but also to introduce them to enjoyable uses that the site will continue to offer after the event is over.

Following is a short list of ideas, just to get you started thinking:

    Grand openings
    Open houses and guided tours
    Crafts demonstrations
    Art and music festivals
    Ethnic events and holiday celebrations
    Unusual sporting events
    Tournaments
    Special Olympics
    Races and walkathons
    Pet shows
    "New games" tournaments
    Celebrations of community or individual achievement
    Puppet shows
    Outdoor community theater productions
    Community picnics
    Holiday celebrations
    Carnivals and fairs
    Parades

Special events must be carefully planned. Begin planning for the event well in advance to leave enough time to overcome the unforeseeable problems that will inevitably occur. Make a list of everything you will need on-site and check and doublecheck your list. Don't overlook seating, P.A. systems, lighting, electrical capability, tickets, clean-up plans, food service, police and traffic control, special permits, waste receptacles, first aid, lost and found, restroom facilities, VIP areas, and an extra vehicle for last-minute emergencies. Identify any celebrity or artisan needs for performances. Assign duties to your staff for the day of the event, making sure that they are adequately trained and capable of their assigned jobs.

Begin arranging advertising, publicity, and other media support two or three months prior to the event. Consider issuing personal invitations to key community leaders, especially those influential with your target group. Consider also arranging for an official proclamation by the city as another means of announcing your upcoming event. Pay special attention to the opening ceremony logistics to assure that your event gets off on the right foot. Assign personnel to assist the media, and arrange for your own photographic coverage.

In order to evaluate the success of your event in efficiently meeting your promotional goals, consider the size of the turn-out, check the financial records, and identify which segments of the public attended. Relate these results to past events, taking into consideration differing weather conditions, conflicting events, and any other external factors which might have significantly impacted attendance. This will give you a good indication of how successful the event was in attracting the audience you sought. However, in most cases the ultimate promotional aim of an event is an increase or change in long-term use patterns. Measuring progress toward meeting such goals may well require detecting subtle trends in use patterns over a long period of time.

Selected Bibliography

ADVERTISING TRADE PUBLICATIONS

<u>Advertising Age</u>, 740 No. Rush St., Chicago, IL 60611, a national weekly magazine all the pros read to keep up to date on marketing, selling, ad campaigns, communications, research and the like.

<u>Art Direction Magazine</u>, 10 East 39th St., New York, NY 10016, focused toward the interests of the visual advertiser - techniques, services and new graphics ideas.

<u>Marketing Communications</u>, 475 Park Ave. So., New York, NY 10016, covers promotions, public relations, direct mail, premiums and advertising media.

<u>Television/Radio Age</u>, 1270 Avenue of the Americas, New York, NY 10020, directed to both buyers and sellers of television and radio time.

GENERAL INFORMATION   (Write to the Publications Department)

The Advertising Council
825 Third Avenue
New York NY   10022

American Business Press, Inc.
205 East 42nd Street
New York, NY   10017

American Marketing Association(AMA)
222 South Riverside Plaza
Chicago, IL   60606

Direct Mail - Marketing Association
6 East 43rd Street
New York, NY   10017

Institute of Outdoor Advertising
485 Lexington Avenue
New York, NY 10017

Newspaper Advertising Bureau
485 Lexington Avenue
New York, NY 10017

Point of Purchase Advertising Institute
60 East 42nd Street
New York, NY 10017

Radio Advertising Bureau
485 Lexington Avenue
New York, NY 10017

Sales Promotion Institute
200 Central Park South
New York, NY 10019

Television Bureau of Advertising, Inc.
1345 Avenue of the Americas
New York, NY 10019

Trendex, Inc.(Research)
800 third Avenue
New York, NY 10022

CONTACTS FOR PROMOTIONAL SEMINARS

GATF
4615 Forbes Avenue
Pittsburgh, PA 15213

Dynamic Graphics
6707 No. Sheridan Road
Peoria, IL 61614

Crain Education Division
740 Rush Street
Chicago, IL 60611